HAUNTED
GARDENS

This book is for my Polish friend
MARLENA SYPNIEWSKA
who has walked with me in
haunted gardens.

First published 2009

Amberley Publishing Plc
Cirencester Road, Chalford,
Stroud, Gloucestershire, GL6 8PE

www.amberley-books.com

Copyright © Peter Underwood, 2009

The right of Peter Underwood to be identified as the
Author of this work has been asserted in accordance
with the Copyrights, Designs and Patents Act 1988.

ISBN 978 1 84868 261 0

British Library Cataloguing in Publication Data.
A catalogue record for this book is available from the
British Library.

Typeset in 11pt on 14pt Celestia Antiqua.
Typesetting and Origination by FONTHILLDESIGN.
Printed in the UK.

HAUNTED GARDENS

An International Journey

by

Peter Underwood

President of The Ghost Club Society
President of The Society for Psychical Studies

AMBERLEY

BY THE SAME AUTHOR

A – Z of British Ghosts (Chancellor)

Dictionary of the Supernatural (Harrap)

Death in Hollywood (Piatkus)

The Ghost Hunters (Robert Hale)

The Ghosts of Borley (David & Charles)

Ghosts of Cornwall (Bossiney)

Ghosts of North Devon (Bossiney)

Ghosts of Somerset (Bossiney)

Guide to Ghosts and Haunted Places (Piatkus)

Haunted London (Harrap)

Jack the Ripper (Blandford)

Karloff – The Life of Boris Karloff (Drake, N.Y.)

Nights in Haunted Houses (Headline)

Short History of The Ghost Club Society (White House Pub.)

This Haunted Isle (Harrap)

Borley Postscript (White House Pub.)

and 30 other titles.

CONTENTS

LIST OF ILLUSTRATIONS

(All are from the author's collection unless otherwise stated)

ACKNOWLEDGEMENTS

The author gratefully acknowledges the generous help and co-operation that he has received from the following: Tom Brown and all the other Ghost Club Society Members who have visited haunted gardens with him; Norman Adams, Robert Aickman, Ernest Ambrose, Juan Armada, Dr Mary Archer, Dennis Bardens, Major D. R. Baxter – Laird of Earlshall, Viola Bayley, Tony Broughall, William Buchan, Dame Barbara Cartland, Derek Chapman, Leslie Charteris, Gerald and Patricia Coke, Fred Cook, Eileen Copes, Tom Corbett, Antony Hippisley Coxe, Pamela and Crispin Derby, James Wentworth Day, Lady Fairfax-Lucy, Dr Joan Evans, Malcolm Forbes, Sir Peter Garran, Jean Paul Getty, Rumer Godden, Robert Graves, Muriel Hankey, Neil Hamilton, G. Howard Heaton, Christina Hole, Lynn Hughes, Michael and Ann Joy, Steuart F. C. Kiernander, Pat Knowles, Dame Cleo Laine, Captain Sandy Livingstone-Learmouth, Ian McCorquodale, Alasdair Alpin MacGregor, Dita Mallet, Eric Maple, Alastair and Elizabeth MacLeod Matthews, James Minahane, Diana Norman, Mary Overgaard, Daniel O'Sullivan, T. Phipps, Dr A. J. B. Robertson, Donald Ross, Dr Peter Hilton Rowe, Charles de Salis, Dorothea St Hill Bourne, Samuel Seal, Arabella Seymour, Tim Smit, James and Jean Le Gendre Starkie, Wilhelmena Stirling, Professor F. J. M. Stratton, S. A. Sursham, Dr Grace Thornton, Chris Underwood, Dudley Ward, Jack Watling, Herbert White, Henry Williamson, together with the administrators, librarians, curators, directors and officials from many organisations but especially the National Trust, English Heritage, Bramshill Police College and The Casemate Museum.

INTRODUCTION

Haunted gardens! Now there's a thought for after the houses we live in – and who can deny there are haunted houses – 'a garden', as Francis Bacon, Viscount St Albans (1561-1626) put it, 'is the purest of human pleasures'; it is also the place where most people spend a great deal of their time, where we toil and rest, live and love, contemplate and remember and recollect; gardens win our hearts and occupy our minds: small wonder that, if something of our thoughts and memories linger on after we are gone, evidence should exist widely in gardens.

One recalls the words of the Scottish author Henry Glassford Bell (1803-1874) in his poem 'Mary Queen of Scots':

> I looked back into other years, and lo! in bright array
> I saw, as in a dream, the forms of ages passed away.
> It was a stately convent, with its old and lofty walls,
> And gardens with their broad, green walks, where soft
> the footstep falls ...

Ghosts are usually seen when least expected; sometimes just the once; sometimes for years and years and sometimes for a while and then no more. Some years ago when John Dankworth and his wife Cleo Laine bought a 150-year-old former rectory in the beautiful Buckinghamshire countryside, they soon realised that the property was haunted, for the ghost of an old man was repeatedly encountered walking about the estate. A girl who worked for them found 'he' suddenly appeared beside her and as unaccountably disappeared; someone else saw 'him' when there was no living person anywhere in the vicinity and Cleo said at the time: 'He must be a nice ghost. If he objected to us or our lifestyle he'd have frightened the daylights out of us by now . . . It is hard to describe his appearance for he's like a vision, a faint impression. He looks like he lived in the nineteenth century and he walks in a way that makes me think he's restless.'

John Dankworth used to laugh at Cleo's claim that she had seen the ghost walking about the grounds; but after friends reported similar eerie sightings he admitted: 'When I saw how scared they were about it I began to believe in him, too. I think he is someone who's been very happy at the old rectory and likes visiting us because it's still a happy place.'

I asked the famous musician and singer couple whether the ghost was still there and in her reply Dame Cleo Laine said: 'We would love to be able to tell you that our apparition is still floating about the garden, but alas we haven't seen hide nor hair for many years. We can only assume that our musical ventures pleased or led him to flee the abode. I think the ghost just wanted to know who the new residents were, and if we were pleasant, musically speaking . . .'

But what is a ghost? Well, as Professor C. E. M. Joad used to say, 'It all depends what you mean' by ghosts. The evidence for ghosts and ghostly activity is formidable, vast and to my mind quite incontrovertible. There are literally thousands and thousands of carefully recorded and often independently witnessed and corroborated experiences from all parts of the world, in all ages and in every kind of civilization. The chances of anyone seeing a ghost sometime during their lifetime is reckoned to be as high as one in ten and the various societies and organisations that have been seriously and scientifically researching this subject for well over a century have collected a mass of remarkably good evidence. In 1998 a MORI poll found that 92 per cent of the population admitted to a belief in the paranormal; and in 1999 ROAR, a market research company, questioned several thousand fifteen to twenty-four-year-olds and 70 per cent declared 'some belief' in ghosts, 61 per cent said they believed in the reality of aliens, while just over 80 per cent felt that the evidence for hauntings was overwhelming.

More than half a century of practical investigation has convinced me that there are several different kinds of ghosts and personally I am not at all sure that the once generally accepted idea that all ghosts are the spirits of the departed bears much examination. It does seem to me that there is overwhelming evidence from all parts of the world that on occasions strong emotions can leave behind 'something' that some people might call a ghost.

This is most often a traumatic experience, a sudden and unexpected calamity or great shock such as sudden death either by accident or design. Conversely great happiness can, it seems, cause 'something' to linger after death, a 'something' that might be called a ghost. There are certainly many instances of the ghostly forms of previous occupants being seen in the house or garden that they loved; quiet, unobtrusive, gentle phantoms that harm no one. It seems indisputable that we can leave something of ourselves behind and we have all experienced this to a degree. We enter a strange house and think – this is a nice house, a really friendly atmosphere, I could live here. In another property we immediately shy away, we don't like the atmosphere, couldn't live there. If we really can leave something of ourselves behind in the place where we live, is it so unlikely that someone, perhaps with a dominant personality, who loves a place almost to distraction, should leave so much of himself or herself at that place that after death others see or sense that person?

Some of the best-known ghosts are in fact historical figures that apparently haunt historical houses and gardens and it is an interesting fact that practically all such ghostly figures pass quietly and purposely through the rooms and passages and gardens that would have been familiar to them in their lifetime. These figures appear to be solid, they act naturally, are seemingly dressed in the clothes of their time but where structural alterations have taken place they appear to walk through hedges, walls and closed doors, and if alterations have been made the ghosts appear where they would have appeared before such alterations took place and so we have ghosts at York and Winchester appearing only from the knees upwards because the flooring has been raised or, as at Cambridge, only the head of a person is seen on the floor of a room, the ceiling of the room having been lowered or altered so that where the ghost now walks it interferes with a new floor. Oddly enough when structural alterations are made in a house it not infrequently disturbs the atmosphere or whatever is conducive to ghostly appearances and a ghost may appear in a previously quiet house or a haunted house may become unhaunted.

I have always thought it interesting that children are good ghost-seers: many children do see ghosts and it may be that before our minds become cluttered with civilisation we are more open and receptive to these matters. In haunted places I and other investigators have sometimes discovered that we will spend hour after hour in serious and complicated investigation with some quite sophisticated equipment and perhaps during the early hours of the morning, having experienced nothing of a supernormal character, we dismantle the equipment and sit back for a little relaxation before packing things up and then disturbances have been reported! It may well be that a relaxed and quiet atmosphere is more conducive and receptive to psychic activity.

Ghosts, it sometimes seems, are concerned with what happened to them, rather than where it happened, although the two often coincide. People who meet premature deaths, be it accident, suicide or murder, often return (if that is the right word) and their forms are seen or heard or felt in the vicinity of the site of the tragedy; and this seems to apply to animals as much as to human beings: in California there is a phantom cow, seemingly mourning the loss of its calf, slaughtered by marauders.

Whether we like it or not there are haunted gardens everywhere we look. In this short volume you are invited to explore with me representative haunted gardens in England, Scotland, Wales, United States of America, France, Spain, Jamaica, Singapore and having done so perhaps you will feel, like me, and with apologies to Dorothy Gurney (1858-1932):

> The kiss of the sun for pardon,
> The song of the birds for mirth,
> One is nearer to ghosts in a garden
> Than anywhere else on earth.

We may not yet know exactly what ghosts are but that they do exist – in as far as they are seen – is beyond argument for anyone who accepts first-hand evidence that would be accepted in a court of law. Ghosts are certainly not figments of the imagination for how can we explain a distinct and individual figure seen at a particular place by different people on different occasions who have no knowledge that such a figure has been seen there before? So what are ghosts? The true answer is we don't know but it seems indisputable that such appearances are seen occasionally by people with healthy minds in healthy bodies. Most ghosts, available evidence would suggest, can be seen by anyone providing that person is in the right frame of mind and in the right place at the right time. And it is always best to be on the safe side, like the sixteenth-century Emperor Maximillian of Austria who frequently called out his army to ensure in advance of his arrival that there were no ghosts in the houses where he was due to stay!

Ghosts – apparitions of dead people or sounds associated with invisible human beings – may well be the surviving emotional memories of people who are no longer present. Perhaps what we are dealing with here is what Dr J. B. Rhine of Duke University described to me as 'the world of the mind'.

'Remember,' someone once said to me, 'a ghost is probably a lonely entity wandering lost in a vast void. One day you too may walk there . . .'

Peter Underwood
Savage Club
1 Whitehall Place
London
SW1A 2HD

ABERGLASNEY HOUSE
Llangathen, Dyfed, Wales

My wife and I made an extended visit to the Principality of Wales in 1977 to explore, investigate and research the haunted places of glorious Wales for my book *Ghosts of Wales*, published by Christopher Davies of Swansea in 1978 and subsequently in paperback by Corgi in 1980.

It was, as I recall, fellow author, playwright and publisher Lynn Hughes who suggested we visit the atmospheric Towy Valley in Carmarthenshire and Joyce and I found ourselves well off the beaten track one sunny July day and we stopped and looked at the overgrown, weed-encrusted and deserted gateway to melancholy and gloom-laden Aberglasney House.

So this was the beautiful and mysterious Towy Valley and this was the once-beautiful Aberglasney House, now silently brooding, full of ghosts and slowly dying in the shadow of Grongar Hill. Since we were there restoration has utterly transformed the place but then much of the masonry was in a dangerous condition. That day I pushed open the rusted iron gates and we made our way through the tangle of grass and weeds and soon found ourselves facing unlucky Aberglasney House, the early home of John Dyer (*c.* 1700-1758), the poet and son of a solicitor, who was born here and it is the view from the 410-foot-high hill that is the subject of his best-known poem, 'Grongar Hill'. In its final form the poem comprises 150 lines and describes in language of much freshness and picturesque charm the view from the hill that overlooks the natural vale of Towy. A visit to Italy in 1740 produced 'The Ruins of Rome', a descriptive piece of some 600 lines of Miltonic blank verse. He was ordained a priest in 1741 and worked in several Lincolnshire parishes. 1757 saw the publication of his longest work, a blank verse epic, 'The Fleece', that discusses the tending of sheep, the shearing and preparation of the wool, the wearing of wool and the trade in woollen manufacture – a thoroughly researched and well written epistle but it is as the author of 'Grongar Hill' that he is best remembered. Wordsworth called him 'the father of nature poetry'.

> Ever charming, ever new,
> When will the landscape tire the view!
> The fountain's fall, the river's flow,
> The woody valleys, warm and low;
> The windy summit, wild and high,
> Roughly rushing to the sky!
> The pleasant seat, the ruined tower,
> The naked rock, the shady bower;
> The town and village, dome and farm,

Each give to each a double charm,
As pearls upon an Ethiop's arm.

It is a gentle masterpiece of a poem by a man who was also a painter; a poem that has been printed in fifty different editions, including *Palgrave's Golden Treasury of Longer Poems* and in each printing there has been an error. All that was eventually put right and the first correct edition, limited to 250 copies was published by the Grongar Press of Llandeilo.

Llangathen churchyard is the last resting place of the generations of Cawdor and Aberglasney tenants and estate workers and there are an unusually large number of infant graves. Here a strange weed has taken hold, a weed that seems to thrive on all known weed-killers, a plant that is fast taking over the graveyard where many corpses lie, it is said, with their feet facing the wrong way – even the effigy of Bishop Anthony Rudd, inside the church, is fashioned with the left hand over the right, sinister over dexter; the hand that should be wearing the episcopal ring of Canterbury covered; and the hands are clasped in prayer.

I have been told that a party of ghost hunters visited Llangathen church on three occasions and each time they found the temperature markedly lower in certain areas and twice they heard the sounds of moans and groans and what sounded like the slamming of a door, although the church door was shut and bolted.

And what of the six young girls whose ghosts walk in the grounds of Aberglasney? Lynn Hughes has researched into the history and legends of this area and he says the girls were maids at the big house who had decorated their bedroom as a surprise for their master and mistress and, sleeping with the doors and windows shut tight, they suffocated from the fumes of lead paint in the Blue Room . . . Now their ghosts walk together with those of the Lords of Gathen and the monks of the vanished abbey that once stood where the hollow-eyed ruin of Aberglasney House nestled that summer day below the hill that made it famous.

History permeates the air about the old house. There was quite a breeze the day we were there, but within the confines of the house and garden all was as quiet and as still as the grave; and my camera, which functioned perfectly before and immediately afterwards, steadfastly refused to give an exposure reading while in the immediate vicinity of Abergasney House.

Many of the high sheriffs of Carmarthenshire in the old days lived here. Sir William Thomas was here in 1545 and probably hunted the youthful Twm Sion Cati in the days when robbers and outlaws infested the area, as they did until the seventeenth century. During the reign of Henry V robbers occupied Aberglasney and are said to have buried treasure in the grounds, gold coins struck in 1340 to commemorate Edward III's victory over the French fleet at Sluys: treasure that has never been found.

In 1594 Anthony Rudd came to Llangathen, acquired Aberglasney and reconsecrated a chapel, still known as Rudd's Chapel; while nearby is a well, probably Roman in origin, called Rudd's Bath House. A famous preacher of his day, Rudd so impressed Elizabeth I that she suggested he succeed Whitgift as archbishop, but jealous men on hearing how things were going surreptitiously advised Rudd, when next he was to preach before the Queen, to cool his enthusiasm as she had grown old and was weary of 'the vanity of wit and eloquence'. Taking the hint, Rudd modulated his performance and delivered a dismal sermon, choosing for his text '0 teach us to number our days' and, somewhat imprudently, implied that 'even the beauty of a queen was subject to the ravages of time'! The Queen was not amused; indeed she took it badly. Rising, she said: 'Enough of your arithmeticking Master Rudd' and he heard no more of Canterbury.

After Rudd's death in 1615, his son, Sir Rice Rudd, spent much time and money in unsuccessful electioneering and eventually became so financially burdened that he was obliged to mortgage Aberglasney; and the Hon Thomas Watson-Wentworth foreclosed on the defaulting Rice Rudd in 1701, having briefed Robert Dyer, a local solicitor, whose baby son was to become the poet John Dyer.

Dyer senior raised the necessary deposit and moved into Aberglasney as a tenant, despite the resistance of Sir Rice; resistance that led to fighting between men who owed allegiance to Rudd and those who supported Dyer. Within a few years Robert Dyer had sold off sections of land to enable him to clear the mortgage but he died in 1720 before actual completion. After a protracted legal action his sons were able to clear up the matter and Aberglasney will always be remembered as the home of one of those sons, John Dyer.

In the middle of the nineteenth century Colonel Meyhew married into the estate and immediately set about exorcising the curse of drink. He closed down the village pub and founded a Temperance Hall with the motto 'Watch and be Sober' emblazoned upon the lintel.

Something of all the varied occupants of Aberglasney House seems to have lingered through the ages. There are those who say they have heard the sound of muffled fighting; those who have heard a mumbled sermon interrupted by the grating of a chair followed by silence; those who have heard the sound of quarrelling and the clink of coins; those who have heard a snatch of a wrathful voice denouncing the devil drink; those who have heard the grumbling voices of discontented tenants; but most of all the quiet sadness of a harmless poet broods over the house, a doom-laden backcloth to the figures of six young girls who wander, silent and aloof, among the growing waist-high weeds that then almost engulfed haunted Aberglasney.

In the 26 December 1998 issue of *Weekend Telegraph* an article caught my eye. Headed 'The Next Heligan' it was written by former Member of Parliament, Neil Hamilton who grew up in Carmarthenshire and used to bicycle around the maze of country lanes. One day in 1963 he tells of chancing upon 'an eighteenth-century gateway half-hidden by ivy and self-seeded saplings'; intrigued, he and a friend pushed their way inside to discover the derelict mansion of Aberglasney.

'The front door was welcomingly open,' he writes. 'Upstairs we picked our way across the dangerous floors to find one room strewn almost knee-high with a maelstrom of paper. We searched among the refuse and filled our saddlebags with modest treasure, returning to our truffle hunt many times during the next few years.'

By 1998 it seemed that Aberglasney was doomed but just as the vandalised house was on the point of collapse, the founder of the Welsh Historic Gardens Trust, William Wilkins, stepped in with a stupendously ambitious plan to restore in particular the haunted garden which, it seems, may well be a unique survival of a complicated medieval Renaissance design.

It has now been established that the eight-acre sloping site comprises a series of rectilinear 'rooms' separated from one another by stone arcades, walls and retaining walls. A large horizontal rectangle at thigh level circumscribes six formal garden compartments and below, a shrub garden leads into the extensive Stream Wood. There is also the Cloister Garden, the Upper Walled Garden, the Lower Walled Garden – and one really exciting feature: a yew tunnel which, with its interconnected mass of gnarled branches, twisted roots and tendrils, looking for all the world like something thought up by Arthur Rackham and his world of witches and goblins. It is estimated to be over a thousand years old and must surely be one of the oldest living garden features in Britain. I asked Neil Hamilton whether he ever had any experience of or

heard anything about the reputed ghosts at Aberglasney but he told me: 'I am very interested . . . and I wish I could add to your stock of anecdotes about ghosts but I am afraid I have never seen or felt anything of this nature at Aberglasney or elsewhere!'

But other visitors have different tales to tell. My friend Donald Ross took the trouble to find Aberglasney House not long after my initial visit and he told me afterwards: 'You told me about six ghostly girls that haunt the place but you did not mention any ghost monks. I saw two walking slowly together near the rough-stone cloister. As I watched they silently passed within about ten feet of me – and then suddenly they were no longer there!' Lynn Hughes, Mary Laurel, John Chapman and various local people and visitors have all reported to me that they have seen ghosts at Aberglasney.

In August 1999 the BBC broadcast a programme entitled 'Aberglasney – A Garden Lost in Time' that related the story of how the old mansion and its weed-choked gardens were painstakingly restored. The house, it was stated, had stood empty since the late fifties, and was already a site of dereliction. What the restorers discovered was a legacy of amazing archaeological finds dating back to the fifteenth-century and many gardening wonders, including a rare yew tunnel hundreds of years old, a Jacobean cloister garden and an ancient cobbled walkway – and all the whole garden area here has been the scene of reported psychic activity.

There are persistent stories of appearances of the six ghostly girls, the phantom Lord of Gathen and monks from the vanished abbey that once stood on the site. There have also been reports within the last few months of the sound of muffled fighting by a party of ladies; a mumbled sermon by a visiting priest; sounds of quarrelling and the clink of coins by a very puzzled antiquarian from France and there have been other mysterious sounds for which no explanation can be found. Restoration, devoted attention, refurbishment and change often triggers psychic activity and with such a wealth and variety of reported activity at Aberglasney, who knows what may occur in the future. Aberglasney is full of history and romance and mystery – and not a few ghosts walk the ancient gardens there.

ALDERTON HALL
Loughton, Essex

A few miles from Epping and under the jurisdiction of Chigwell, Loughton boasts many modern public and industrial buildings, including the Bank of England printing works, but it also contains a fifteenth-century former farmhouse, Alderton Hall, and local people – since time immemorial it seems – have believed that the house and in particular the gardens are haunted.

One of the stories concerned a squire at the Hall in the 1750s who seduced a young maidservant and, when she became pregnant, he denied everything, married someone of his own class, and turned the servant and her baby out of the house. Utterly miserable she drowned herself and her baby in a nearby pool. Some versions of the story say that when the squire's wife had a son the nanny had charge of the toddler one day near the fatal pool when the child pointed at the water, mumbling something about a baby, before the nanny's eyes 'something' materialised from the pool and seemed to pull the child into the water and he was drowned.

From 1957 to 1981 actor Jack Watling and his family lived at the timbered house and many and frequent were the reports of ghosts all the years they were there; not that they were unduly worried on the whole, although there were exceptions, as we shall see. In 1991 Jack Watling, from his home at Frinton on Sea told me, 'We had many happy years at the Hall and our experiences there only enriched our lives.'

My good friend and Ghost Club Society member Eric Maple, who spent a lifetime investigating witchcraft and ghostology, talked at length with Jack Watling and his family at the haunted house and learned much at first-hand about the ghosts and the haunting. Jack Watling, apart from three years in the RAF, was employed all his working life in stage, film and television work and is the father of three daughters, Dilys, Debbie and Nikki, and a son, Giles; both Dilys and Debbie have inherited their father's acting talents. Related Jack Watling: 'When we first moved into Alderton Hall I didn't take much notice of the stories told about ghosts but subsequent events made me change my mind.' Twice the actor heard invisible fingers running along the keys of his piano, among other apparently inexplicable happenings, including strange and unexplained figures and forms in the garden; and the other occupants of the house have their own stories.

Actress Debbie awoke one night in her bedroom (which soon became known as 'the haunted bedroom') to find a face peering intently down at her. It was a girl with old-fashioned hairstyle and a very pale complexion. Then Debbie felt her hand clasped by another hand. Thinking she was dreaming she sat up – and was amazed to see the distinct figure of a young girl leave the bedside, walk across the room and disappear into a solid wall! Debbie told Eric Maple that she was only about eight years old when she first began to hear footsteps and strange noises, inside and outside the house. Her room certainly seemed to be the most haunted and she and her father wondered whether that was once the maid's room; the girl who had been deceived. Often Debbie would hear her name called and once she saw a girl's face on the wall. It was very life-like and looked intently at her for a few seconds and then completely disappeared. She wasn't at all frightened but remembers just thinking, 'What a pretty face . . .' In fact she was never really frightened at Alderton Hall, 'It's as if it was all part of the property' she said – and yet, the bedroom door was very heavy, solid oak, with a large latch that needed considerable pressure to get it open but this door frequently opened all by itself, 'with all the creaks and groans of a horror film!' Time after time Debbie tried to fling it open in the hope of coming face to face with whoever or whatever opened the door but she was never successful in seeing anyone or anything that had caused the door to open. Later Debbie talked of seeing things flying around her bedroom, the lights flickering on and off, figures in the garden and 'something' grabbing her by the arm and dragging her several yards before releasing her; something invisible but immensely strong.

Nikki recalled the time when she and Debbie shared a bedroom as children and were awakened one night by an almighty crashing sound. Nikki said she jumped out of bed and turned on the light thinking an article of furniture in the room had fallen on its face. Instead she found everything on the bedside table had been swept right across the room. It was just as though some powerful but invisible hand had swept the entire contents from the bedside table across the room to crash against the wall; and all the books in the bookcase had been flung about the room. Furthermore in the morning the sisters found to their astonishment that their heavy oak double bed had been moved in the night several feet away from the wall, its accustomed position, although neither girl had been aware of any movement of the bed.

Their brother Giles had experiences of his own and more than once he saw the figure of a girl in white who vanished as he stared at her. This happened once in an attic room in the house and once in the garden. On both occasions Giles was certain it was the same girl but the mystery of what she was doing when he saw her and how she disappeared in front of his eyes were problems he never solved.

Alderton Hall has its secrets: there is a hidden passage that served as an air-raid shelter during the Second World War and a bricked-up fireplace which is associated with a story of a highwayman, Dick Turpin himself no less, according to what an earlier owner told Jack Watling. The story goes that wicked Dick Turpin, who in reality was entirely without scruples or mercy, used the fireplace to roast an old woman until she revealed where she had hidden her money; and the ghost of the old woman – not Dick Turpin in this instance, although his ghost reputedly appears elsewhere in Essex, especially in Epping Forest, north of Loughton, on Hounslow Heath, in the Midlands between Hinckley and Nuneaton and in the vicinity of Woughton on the Green in Buckinghamshire – has been seen, sometimes outside the house itself and at other times near the fireplace inside the house.

In the garden and drive of Alderton Hall Jack Watling saw, more than once, the distinct figure of a fair-haired man wearing a red cloak. The form stood for a moment, apparently solid and real in every way, looking at the house and then, as the owner watched, the figure suddenly vanished. On both occasions Jack Watling immediately searched the area but found no one and nothing to account for what he had seen. Jack Watling described the figure to me as 'a cavalier-like figure that stood behind my wife; she turned and saw him too before he disappeared'. Afterwards Jack Watling learned that other people had seen the figure of a man wearing a red cape in the garden; a man with fair hair, but who he was and why he haunted no one seemed to know.

Debbie summed up the approach by the Watling family to the mysterious events they encountered at Alderton Hall when she said, 'We never attempted to seriously investigate the hauntings with apparatus or cameras or anything like that. We felt it would be a dreadful invasion . . . we all managed to live there quite peacefully, ghosts and humans, and there was always a really friendly atmosphere'.

Once, Jack Watling saw the fair-haired man swathed in a long red cloak standing in the drive; when he ran out to see who it was and what he wanted, there was no one there. Thinking back Jack Watling wondered whether this could be the wicked squire looking for the girl he had so grievously wronged.

The house might well retain in some way some of the traumatic happenings that took place there centuries ago but how could the garden do that? Could some kind of image persist in the atmosphere that reactivates and reappears under certain conditions, perhaps climatic conditions or the presence of certain people (three young girls and a boy perhaps); a kind of vision that is only visible from a particular vantage point and disappears when approached or receded from?

BADDESLEY CLINTON HALL
Baddesley Clinton, near Warwick, Warwickshire

Described by S. P. B. Mais as 'one of the most charmingly picturesque fifteenth-century domestic buildings in all England', Baddesley Clinton Hall has changed little since 1634 and this romantically-sited, medieval, moated manor house, standing in 120 acres, is deservedly haunted both inside and outside.

There has long been a tradition that Guy Fawkes (1570 -1606) once lived at Baddesley Clinton and in 1604, the year of the abortive Gunpowder Plot, the Hall was owned and occupied by the steadfastly Catholic Ferrers family who adhered to the Old Religion after the Reformation. In fact the owner at that time was Henry Ferrers (1549 -1633) and he inherited when he was only fourteen and remained in possession for nearly seventy years, although he was away for long periods. In 1589 he bought a house in Westminster, next to the Houses of Parliament and the fortuitous position of this property resulted in his playing – possibly unwittingly – a part in momentous events, for he assigned the lease of the house to Thomas Percy, one of the Gunpowder plotters and it was there that Guy Fawkes stored the barrels of gunpowder.

'The True Copy of the Declaration of Guido Fawkes' (who originally gave his name as John Johnson) states that it was for the express purpose of hiding the twenty barrels of powder that Thomas Percy 'hired a house at Westminster . . . near adjoining to the Parliament House' and there began to make plans about 11 December 1604; plans that all but came to fruition – as every schoolboy knows – on 5 November 1605.

Whether or not Guy Fawkes lived at Baddesley Clinton is open to speculation and my old friend Glanville Squiers, of *Secret Hiding Places* fame, told me that since there is no evidence that the house was ever used by the Gunpowder Plot conspirators, he thought it quite likely that the names of Fawkes and Vaux (a devout Catholic family who did live at Baddesley Clinton for a while), which are pronounced the same except for the initial letter, had become confused over the years. The lantern said to have belonged to Guy Fawkes is not at Baddesley Clinton but is preserved in the Bodleian Library at Oxford.

Glanville Squiers, incidentally, was fascinated by Baddesley Clinton Hall and its secret hiding places and as a keen ghost enthusiast thought there might well be a connection between the priests' hiding places and the ghosts that haunt the place. His feeling for the place is evident from his introductory paragraph in his book (*Secret Hiding Places*, Stanley Paul, 1934): 'Baddesley Clinton is one of the best preserved of our English mansions, both inside and out. It is built mainly of stone – with a wing of red brick – and consists of three wings built round a courtyard and surrounded by a moat. It is not a particularly large house, but it is a gem of beauty, set in perfect surroundings.'

Granville Squiers discovered and examined a wealth of secret hiding places at Baddesley Clinton including a tunnel, at the base of the west or back wing which runs the entire length of the wing and is lighted by loopholes before it exits into the moat. The present guidebook to the house refers to this as the medieval sewer. Incidentally the West Side contained the best accommodation and was reserved for John Brome and his family whom we shall meet a little later. Glanville Squiers says this former sewer was afterwards converted into a hiding place for two undoubted secret ways that have been made into it. One entrance is via a window seat in the Blue Bedroom, formerly The Priest's Room. Another priest hole is situated in the roof, amongst the chimneys on the south side of the gate tower. Within there is ample seating room for six people. In the corner of the kitchen is a glass panel in the floor and below this panel is another priest's hole. Nicholas Owen, the great constructor of secret hiding places, appears to have constructed at least three at Baddesley Clinton. The present guidebook tells of Father Garnet, the Jesuit Superior, and his fellow Catholics hiding there for over four hours in October 1591. Nicholas Owen and Father Garnet were later caught, tortured and executed, after being accused of complicity in the Gunpowder Plot.

On the death of Nicolas Brome in 1517 the property was inherited by Sir Edward Ferrers who had married Brome's daughter and co-heir, Constance. Baddesley Clinton Hall then passed from father to son in a direct line for twelve generations, until it was sold, in 1980, to the government, which conveyed it to the National Trust.

And this Nicholas Brome may well have much to do with one of the hauntings at Baddesley Clinton. In Tudor times the battlemented and indeed spectacular house was the home of the Brome family for many years. Three times married, Nicholas was the violent member of the family and is on record as having committed at least two murders. The first occurred when the property was in the possession of one John Brome, a lawyer who flourished in the reign of Henry VI. Brome was killed in London in a dispute with a man named Herthill over a mortgage, a death that was avenged by Nicholas for three years later he waylaid Herthill and attacked him so fiercely that he later died. Nicholas Brome was required to do penance for this act and he did that which was required of him. However, his troubles were not over, for on his return home unexpectedly one day in 1485, he discovered his domestic chaplain in compromising circumstances with his wife and, being a man of hasty temper, Brome slew the priest on the spot; and so he was in serious trouble with the Church yet again. This time, by way of expiation, he had to embellish the parish church at Baddesley Clinton and erect a new steeple for the church at Packwood.

Nicholas Brome died in 1517, a man weary of this life, but whether it is his ghost or that of the priest he murdered – or possibly both – that haunts the old manor house and even older garden is not known; but the haunting was sufficiently well authenticated at one time, or sufficiently well-known, to be included in Charles Harper's classic work on haunted houses, published in 1907.

As one author has put it, 'It would hardly be surprising if a man so maniacally attached to his family and property did not remain in his ancestral home, in spirit, for as long as possible' and it could well be the shade of the murderous Nicholas Brome himself who has regularly been seen lurking in the dark corners of this secluded mansion or hastening along one of the ancient paths in the gardens.

In the long history of the house and in recent years there have been many reported manifestations of ghosts both inside the atmospheric Hall and outside in the enjoyable gardens. The moat-side path leading to the Great Pool seems a favourite haunt but there have also been reported 'presences' in the Walled Garden and in the Wild Flower Meadow. Stories of the sound of muttered argument and disagreement between several men; shadowy and silent forms that are there one minute and gone the next; footsteps, some stealthy and slow and others quick and fleeting, sometimes light and difficult to hear and at other times heavy, distinct and leisured; have all repeatedly been reported from many parts of the house and grounds. There has also been unexpected movement of objects and, frequently reported, a heavy atmosphere that can be completely overwhelming. One lady was 'so oppressed by the atmosphere' in the Library that she had to leave the room immediately and another lady 'encountered an invisible but distinctly tangible' presence on one of the ancient paths that sent her speeding back to the house.

Interestingly enough the Library was, in medieval times, a first-floor chamber adjoining the low end of the Great Hall that used to occupy the north side of the courtyard, and may well have accommodated a steward. Henry Ferrers, known as 'the Antiquary', believed this to be the room where Nicholas Brome murdered the Baddesley priest and the indelible bloodstain in front of the fireplace has long been taken as proof of this. Subsequently the chamber became a bedroom and, due to the repeated appearance there of a ghostly female form, it became known as 'The Ghost Room'.

The ghosts at Baddesley Clinton seem to have a habit of manifesting themselves to visitors and in 1884, according to a diary kept by a member of the Ferrers family, a lady visitor awoke in the middle of the night to see the figure of a fair-haired woman, dressed in black, in the bedroom. She glided past the bed and vanished through a closed door. Three years later the same lady visited Baddesley Clinton again and, although on this occasion she occupied a different room, she again experienced a disturbed night, again finding herself suddenly awake and again seeing the figure of a woman, the same form she had seen previously, this time clearly in the bright moonlight that flooded into the room. This time the form was standing beside a writing desk and facing the bed. Her features, the visitor decided, had a definite resemblance to members of the Ferrers family. After a moment the figure vanished.

It seems that other people, visitors, employees and residents, have seen a similar figure, usually in the upper parts of the house but occasionally in one of the corridors – where a visiting clergyman encountered the ghost seemingly sitting in a chair; but a moment later she had vanished – and also occasionally in the walled garden.

Whether this phantom form is that of a member of the Ferrers family has never been definitely established but another ghost here does seem to be a Ferrers, the family so long associated with Baddesley Clinton. Major Thomas Ferrers died in an accident abroad and seventy years after his death his ghost was seen and recognised from a portrait by a guest in the house. On a second visit this guest saw the same form again, this time seemingly surrounded by a gilt frame – almost like a picture – and the whole appearance was superimposed on one of the pictures hanging in the room. A similar ghostly experience was reported some years later in the Blue Room by a visitor who had no knowledge of the history of the house or its reputed ghosts. The Blue Room, situated on the first floor, next to Henry Ferrer's bedroom on one side and the sacristy and Chapel on the other, was the room where visiting priests would sleep and could well have once been occupied by the flirtatious priest who was murdered in the act of philandering.

The unexplained sound of footsteps, muttering, rapping and tapping sounds and the noise of cloth being torn do seem to have been reported from inside and outside Baddesley Clinton for years. Almost a century ago a guest, Mrs Henrietta Knight, spent an eventful and frightening night here, the kind of night that has been reported by other people including those on a first visit and with no knowledge whatever of the house or any previous experiences of strange happenings. Mrs Knight was awakened from a deep slumber by the sound of loud footsteps on the stairway and passage outside her room. She said afterwards that they were of such volume and variety that she judged there must be at least four or five people involved. Eventually the sounds faded and then ceased altogether but just when Mrs Knight breathed a sigh of relief she heard a tapping sound emanating from the walls and then from the flooring of the room. The taps increased in volume and rapidity only to abruptly cease and be replaced by the frightening sound of cloth being torn, first from one area of the room and then from another. After a moment this too ceased and she heard the sound of breathing and this too was very frightening for it appeared to be very near at hand. Hardly daring to breathe herself she lay and listened until eventually this sound too ceased and to her immense relief was not replaced by any sound and the rest of the night she was undisturbed but lay for hours wondering whether something else was going to occur; this did not result in her getting a restful night and in the morning she left Baddesley Clinton as soon as she could decently do so. Oddly enough she did take a quick walk in the quiet garden early in the morning and was astonished to find herself surrounded by invisible muttering people; as she turned to hurry back indoors she was accompanied by a gasping sound as of someone, invisible, who had exerted themselves almost to the limit of their capability. No wonder she was more than a little pleased to leave Baddesley Clinton with its ghosts behind her.

The administrator at Baddesley Clinton in the early 1970s told me about two further incidents and he supplied me with the names and addresses of the people concerned. Some forty years ago the ghost of a priest was reportedly seen celebrating Mass in the Chapel. The spectral form was seen to remove vestments or something from a box and deposit whatever it was on top of a box in the sacristy. No reason or historical fact has ever been discovered for this curious ghostly performance, but perhaps it had something to do with the murdered chaplain for he does seem to have left behind some psychic influence that is evident from the second incident. This concerned a visitor who was about to enter the solar but discovered that he was unable to do so because of an overwhelming feeling of an unseen presence in the immediate vicinity. This visitor was completely unaware of the murder here in 1485.

There is also a ghost story associated with another room at Baddesley Clinton. This concerns a member of the family who owned the house at the time of Waterloo, Edward Ferrers. He was a soldier, and being killed in battle apparently did not receive Christian burial and, perhaps for that reason, his ghost has appeared, I am reliably informed, on more than one occasion, to people sleeping in his bedroom. Following a special Mass, 'after entreating the Pope, his soul was comforted and he did not appear again'.

Some years ago Mr G. Howard Heaton told me that fifty years earlier when he was a young man he spent a good deal of time at Baddesley Clinton and in those days the house was occasionally opened in aid of the Red Cross. He continued: 'I, who knew the place well, acted as guide to parties of the visiting public and on several occasions when we passed out of the Chapel into the small closet adjoining, we would find a set of priest's vestments lying on the floor, as if they had been cast off in a hurry. Once, when I mentioned this to the then owner (this was before the property passed to the National Trust), she told me she had had a similar experience herself and added that she had been into the room in question that morning when everything had been in order. These vestments were kept in a large bow-fronted chest of drawers in the room, so that they could lie unfolded. The theory is that in the days of the persecution of the Catholics, if a priest was celebrating Mass when government troops or officials arrived, he would leave as quickly as possible; and in such a case of urgency he would discard his vestments and use a ladder in the passage under the room, leading to the passage on the ground floor and then he would flee across the moat through the secret opening in the wall. These passages are still open, I believe, and I have been inside them all in those far-off days.'

A few years ago I was again invited down to beautiful Baddesley Clinton and there in front of television cameras I recounted some of the ghost encounters and strange happenings that have occurred there. As I sat in the Great Hall where so much of great moment has happened, a room known to so many men and women over the past 500 years, or in the Library with its everlasting bloodstain, or in the haunted bedroom, the years seemed to fall away and for a moment all was as it had been long, long ago. Returning to Baddesley Clinton was like going home after a long time away for it is a truly romantic, atmospheric and utterly delightful place, so full of memories – and not a few ghosts.

BATTLE ABBEY
East Sussex

The great abbey at Battle was founded by William the Conqueror to commemorate his victory over King Harold in 1066 and is supposed to have been built on the actual spot where the battle was fought. At the exact spot where Harold fell with an arrow in his eye and the gem-studded standard was captured, a high altar was built within the abbey church, but all that now remains to mark the site is a fir tree and here the famous 'bloody fountain' is still said to spring up after a shower, a sign to the credulous of the immense efflux of blood that was shed hereabouts. The 'fountain of blood' is still reported to me from time to time as is, curiously enough, and despite the scepticism of some people, the ghostly figure of Harold himself, complete with arrow embedded in one of his eyes and dripping blood ... but by far the commonest ghost hereabouts is that of a monk in a brown or butter-coloured habit. Most commonly seen in the vicinity of the fourteenth-century abbey gateway the figure invariably moves with a gliding motion and the face is hidden in a cowl. Sometimes the phantom form is accompanied by sound: shuffling footsteps or a loud rustling as might be expected by a trailing habit, and at other times the form is seen without any accompaniment of sound.

There have also been reports of a mysterious lady dressed in a long red dress, seemingly Elizabethan; and also a limping lady in a grey dress: both have been reportedly seen here within the last few years and the monk has been seen according to reliable reports over many years and as recently as 1999. The figure was especially active, by all accounts, when the church was damaged by fire and when there was an outbreak of vandalism resulting in flooding.

The frequent appearance of the ghost monk around the time of damage by fire and water is especially interesting in view of the legend of Battle Abbey.

At the time of the dissolution of the monasteries Battle Abbey was given by Henry VIII to Sir Anthony Browne and the last of the departing monks turned and cursed the new owner for generation after generation until the line perished by fire and water. Sir Anthony's other property in Sussex, Cowdray House, was indeed gutted by fire but not until 250 years later, in 1793, and around the same time the last Lord Montague,

Battle Abbey.

John Pulsford, Eastbourne. Printed in Prussia.

then a young man, was drowned while failing to negotiate the falls at Schaffhausen on the Rhine. The story goes that messengers hurrying from England to inform his lordship of the great fire that had gutted his house and destroyed all its treasures met other messengers on their way to England with news of the death of the young lord. For years part of the grounds at Cowdray were known as 'The Lady's Walk', on account of the ghostly appearances of Lady Montague who remained true to the fifth Viscount although he shot a priest at the altar because he had dared to begin Mass without waiting for the presence of his lordship who had to flee into hiding from which he emerged from time to time to meet his wife in the park.

Antony Hippisley Coxe, who knew a thing or two about ghosts, once told me that while staying at Battle Abbey as a boy he was told that a ghostly friar haunted the Monks' Walk, although a later owner told Antony that she believed the ghost was not a monk or a friar but the phantom form of the Duchess of Cleveland, to whom the abbey was let for a time, making her way to church. She it was who, in her 1887 History of Battle, wrote that so much work was required to clear up after visitors' 'rural feasts' on the former battlefield that she and the duke decided to lock the gates. This paranormal presence would possibly tie in with the sound of rustling, as of a long dress, that has long been reported in this area when nothing is visible.

James Minahane of St Leonards-on-Sea has sent me the following account of a daylight visit to Battle Abbey in 1963. He adds the information in a subsequent letter that the weather was perfect and his mother was long-sighted, very truthful and teetotal(!).

'I returned to England from abroad in 1963 together with my mother and we settled in the Hastings area. One hot and sunny day in August, we visited Battle Abbey for the first time, and as it was lunchtime we found ourselves alone on the below-ground site of the abbey, and a few yards from where Harold fell.

'Noticing a walk bordered by yew trees along the high boundary wall, I went down it to see where it led, while my mother stood outside it on the lawn. I remember feeling a chill when halfway down the path, which surprised me as it was such a warm and sunny day. The walk came to a dead end so I returned along it back to where my mother was standing but now wearing an astonished expression. She asked me what had become of the other people who had been walking the path with me. I said, truthfully, that I had been alone. She then told me this story.

'After I had gone over halfway and was passing out of sight, I was replaced by two figures coming in the opposite direction. At first, she thought them to be young women in long skirts as she saw these rising and falling as the pair advanced into full view. As they came nearer she could see that they were monks, the nearside one being dressed in an off-white or butter-coloured habit and the far-side one in a dark habit. Their cowls were not in view. They were benign in appearance and spoke in cultured voices. Their ages she could only guess as being in their early thirties. One thing stood out. They were having a difference of opinion so their words were not discernable, and they spoke on top of each other, each waving his arms a little to emphasise his points. Yet they remained in character as benevolent gentleman – if a little irritated!

'Every detail of their dress and persons was clear. The off-white one was the shorter and heavier of the two and he had long, ginger hair. The monk in the dark habit had dark hair and a paler complexion. Their whole figures from crown to sandals were clearly delineated and there was nothing hazy or indistinct about them. Still arguing, they strolled past my mother to the end of the path where they vanished abruptly and the sound of their voices ceased at the same time. They had been in view for several minutes.

'My mother had the whole scene in view and there was absolutely nowhere they could have gone. I had another good vantage point inside the walk and neither saw nor heard anything. All this was against the twelve-foot-high perimeter wall while on the other side there was a fifty-foot drop to the road below. They should have emerged into an open area with an asphalt path where there was no cover. They were never out of her sight while on the walk.

'I questioned her many times and she always kept to the same story. We found no explanation. We had had all the "escape" routes in full view, and they were "surrounded". There was no loophole where humans could have slipped through. Everybody, including ourselves, was in full sunshine and we searched the whole area. About half an hour later an after-lunch party arrived in charge of a guide. He pointed scornfully to the same path and said that ghosts had been reported there but in his opinion the spirits seen had some connection with those that were to be found in bottles. We said nothing.

'Neither of us has ever had any psychic experience and had not gone there anticipating such events. We were on holiday and were relaxed. Later I looked up the abbey's history and found that it had been inhabited by the Black Benedictines who had been suppressed by Henry VIII. The path is shown on old maps as 'Monks' Walk' or 'Ghosts' Walk'. We had not known this. We never found an explanation for the experience but we would like this story to be recorded and preserved somewhere for it is all true.'

During my many visits to Battle over the years – we nearly bought an ancient cottage there many years ago – I always kept an eye open for ghosts in the vicinity of Battle Abbey and once I thought I saw one. It was near the enormous gateway and as my wife and I approached one glorious, sunny summer afternoon we both noticed simultaneously a monk-like figure also approaching the gateway. We slackened the speed of our approach to allow him to precede us and, with cowl up (although as I say it was a hot and sunny afternoon) so we could discern no features, the figure hurried on and reached the gateway some twenty yards or so ahead of us; he turned into the gateway – and completely vanished! We could hardly believe our eyes and immediately sought a logical explanation but there was no way he could have gone without our seeing him.

Had we seen the ghost monk that has haunted the vicinity of Battle Abbey for many, many years? Looking back on the incident neither of us remembered hearing any sound accompanying the manifestation – if manifestation it was!

BORLEY RECTORY (SITE)
Borley, Essex

Borley Rectory, 'the most haunted house in England' – what thoughts and memories the name still conjures up! More than seventy years have passed since the ugly, red-brick house on the hill was destroyed by fire and subsequently dismantled and sold brick by brick until nothing of the most famous of all haunted houses remained above ground level. The former rectory land has long ago been sold off and built upon and the actual site of the rambling old rectory is no longer visible and yet the story of the alleged haunting and the people who lived there lives on – there is even a Borley Rectory Society with its own website.

The whole story of Borley and its ghosts has been the subject of seven full-length books and scores of references in numerous other books; there have been television and radio programmes (some of which I have taken part in myself); there have been innumerable articles and lectures; dozens of public and private debates have presented or questioned the evidence and an awesome number of people have spent an astonishing number of man-hours describing or attempting to debunk the testimony. I first visited the site and haunted garden in 1947 and I was there in 2008, visiting old friends. Between those dates, during those sixty years, I visited the place

on many, many occasions, staying at the cottage (still there but modernised out of all recognition) with James and Cathy Turner and after they left staying at The Bull, Long Melford. I also went there for the purpose of filming with Pathé or the BBC or independent companies; for conducting investigations on the site and in the church; taking part in Ghost Club Society visits or simply visiting a fascinating part of the English countryside – and between whiles contacting, and in most cases personally interviewing, practically everyone who had ever had anything to do with this curious and seemingly never-ending instance of spontaneous paranormal activity.

Briefly, Borley Rectory was built by the Rev H. D. E. Bull in 1863 (I have in my possession one of the original carved boundary stones) on the site of the former Herringham rectory. H. D. E. Bull died in the Blue Room at Borley Rectory in 1892 and was succeeded as rector by his son the Rev Harry Bull (I have an inkwell he carved in the shape of a walnut). He, in turn, died in the Blue Room in 1927 (some say helped on his way by his wife, a Roman Catholic: certainly the pair lived in disharmony and on his marriage Harry's unmarried sisters moved out of their home). Harry was one of fourteen children and I met some of the surviving brothers and sisters, including Ethel, Constance and Alfred who always welcomed me to their later home Chilton Lodge, Great Cornard, and Alfred gave me a framed photograph of himself as a young naval cadet. Ethel was one of the three Bull sisters who saw the famous Borley Nun one afternoon in the rectory garden. The sisters were returning from a garden party on 28 July 1900. As they entered the lower gate (removed and sold some years ago) they all saw at a distance of perhaps a hundred yards the dark figure of a nun slowly gliding rather than walking away from the rectory towards the bottom of the garden at the edge of the lawn that became known as 'The Nun's Walk'. The sisters were terrified – although they hardly knew why but there was something very frightening about the silent figure but that the three of them saw the figure collectively there can be no doubt. While two of them remained watching, the third sister ran into the house and fetched another sister who also saw the figure (but from a different vantage point) and refusing to believe there was anything strange about the seemingly solid figure, she moved forward to address the intruder whereupon the figure stopped, turned to face the rectory and then vanished! For the rest of their lives, over fifty years, the four sisters told identical and consistent stories of the experience.

Following the death of Harry Bull, Eurasian Guy Eric Smith became rector of Borley and he and his newly-married wife experienced such a wealth of strange happenings (taps from a mirror, keys shooting out of locks, articles appearing from nowhere, bell-ringing, clock hands moving inexplicably, shadowy forms, rooms that lit up by themselves, whisperings, a phantom coach and the inevitable footsteps) that he wrote to a national newspaper who contacted Harry Price, at that time the world's leading psychic investigator. Years later, after the death of her husband and twenty years after leaving Borley, Mrs Smith told a different story when interviewed by Mrs K. M. Goldney who has been described as having 'a steam-roller personality and more than capable of convincing anyone that they did not see what they had in fact seen'. The Smiths lasted nine months and were succeeded by the Rev Lionel Foyster, a cousin of the Bulls, and his much younger wife Marianne, with whom I was in touch for some years.

There followed a truly extraordinary five years when apparent phenomena of practically every description ever experienced took place inside the house and outside in the rectory garden. The myriad of extraordinary happenings were witnessed by dozens of people from all walks of life. After the Foysters left the ecclesiastical authorities decided that the place was not suitable for the clergy, the living of Borley was combined with that of nearby Liston and the rector of both parishes lived at Liston Rectory. This new rector was in fact the Rev Alfred Henning who used Borley Rectory from time to time, experienced strange happenings in the house and in the garden and became so interested in the haunting that he produced a booklet called *Haunted Borley* and he became friendly with Harry Price who rented Borley Rectory for a year and organised scientific investigations that broke new ground in the study of haunted houses.

When he learned that Borley Rectory was to be sold, Harry Price, who had extensively explored the mysteries of Borley and eventually produced two books on the subject, asked whether he could have the Great Bell that H. D. E. Bull had hung high up in the courtyard when the house was built. For years it hung outside Price's workshop at his home in Pulborough, Sussex, and on his death the executors of the estate and the University of London presented it to me and it now resides in my garden where I am still waiting for it to ring by paranormal means!

Borley Rectory was bought by Captain W. H. Gregson and during his ownership the fire occurred that saw the end of Borley Rectory. Two later owners of the site, a Mr Woods and Captain Russell, disposed of everything that escaped the fire, even down to the bricks; but still 'something' seems to linger at Borley.

A brief resume of unexplained happenings in the garden at Borley Rectory serve to establish that here was indeed a haunted garden with its Nun's Walk skirting the lawn on the south side where the unexplained figure of a nun has reportedly been seen on numerous occasions by residents, local people, visitors and even ghost hunters – as we shall see. In addition the phantom form of a male person in a long coat or cloak, a monk possibly or a groom, was seen in the otherwise deserted and moonlit courtyard by Edward Cooper who lived in the cottage with his wife for four years during the incumbency of the Rev Harry Bull as he and his wife told me in the presence of witnesses many years later. Once, not long after they had moved into the cottage, Cooper saw a 'Sister of Mercy' (as he called her) emerging from the back entrance of the rectory; at the same time he saw the Rev Harry Bull following the figure. He joined the rector and they followed the silent figure at a distance of some six yards – no more, he assured me – and when 'she' reached the roadway 'she' suddenly and inexplicably disappeared.

Among visitors to Borley Rectory at this time were Mr P. Shaw Jeffrey, former headmaster of Colchester Royal Grammar School, who claimed to see the nun several times during visits to the rectory. I was in touch with Shaw Jeffrey (who died in 1952) and he confirmed that he had seen the nun and in all the years that followed he never denied or retracted or even modified his previous evidence. He had been a fellow student with Harry Bull at Oxford. Then there was Ernest Ambrose, organist at Borley for seventeen years, who told me he had personal experience of paranormal activity in the garden at Borley Rectory and he had spoken to no less than a dozen people who had caught a glimpse of something like a nun on the lawn at Borley. He said the rector's sisters talked about the apparition in quite casual terms and pointed out to him the path and lawn where they had seen the ghost; when he asked them what they felt about the ghost, they said, 'Oh, we are quite used to it. It doesn't bother us at all'. They talked about the nun always appearing on 28 July, the date they had first seen her. He told me all the Bull sisters were very down to earth, not given to exaggeration or emotionalism, nor inclined to search for the supernatural. They were absolutely convinced they had seen the ghost nun on several occasions and they just accepted it as a plain fact.

Another Oxford friend of Harry Bull who became an army officer told me he used to visit the rectory and play tennis with Harry and his sisters. He said it was common to find Harry, anytime between 10.00 p.m. and 3.00 a.m. during the summer months, in the summer house facing the Nun's Walk, hoping to see the ghostly figure – which he did, apparently, on occasions. Yet another Oxford friend told me Harry's wife was not particularly interested in the ghost but appeared to take the haunt, including the 'existence' of the nun for granted. Another Oxford friend of Harry described him to me as one of the most normal of men you could meet; this particular friend became a doctor and practised on the Isle of Wight; he had visited Borley Rectory and heard all about the ghost nun which the whole family seemed to accept.

In 1929, on the occasion of Harry Price's initial visit to Borley when he was accompanied by Mr V. C. Wall, both gentlemen thought they saw a shadow or something moving along the Nun's Walk. Before leaving the early reports of paranormal activity in the precincts of Borley Rectory we must consider the amazing story of the phantom coach and horses as related by the Coopers.

One night, soon after dawn, the Coopers awoke to see what they could only describe as a 'black shape' running round their bedroom – before they had time to do anything it had vanished. Another night Edward Cooper thought he heard something in the courtyard below their bedroom at the back of the cottage and looking out of his bedroom window he saw, 'clearly and unmistakably' (he told me) a black coach drawn by two horses; its lamps blazing and the harness glittering in the bright moonlight. A rather dim figure sat on the box and as he peered at the curious sight, he called his wife to come and look but by the time his wife reached the window the coach had silently passed out of the courtyard going in the direction of the church, just across the road, and Mrs Cooper saw nothing on that occasion. Cooper always said that Harry Price had described the incident incorrectly, saying it passed through a hedge and into the farmyard. 'They got it a bit muddled in the book,' the Coopers told me as they told Brigadier C. A. L. Brownlow, for the coach had in fact proceeded in the opposite direction. When he was told that it was mistakes such as that which caused some people to cast doubt on the whole haunting, Cooper smiled and said he could not vouch for the whole Borley story but he and his wife stuck to their own testimony; they knew what they had seen. The Coopers, it has to be said, always gave a consistent account of their experiences, while they were at Borley and at nearby Sudbury where they moved in 1920 and lived for the rest of their lives. I interviewed them in August 1954.

The Rev H. D. E. Bull (1833-1892) and his wife certainly knew all about the legendary ghostly nun and indeed they are credited with having the large summer house in the garden, facing the Nun's Walk, built for the express purpose of watching for her appearances; and having a window in the dining-room bricked-up for some such reason as the sight of a ghost disturbing the dining habits of his family. At all events it was during the occupancy of the Rev Henry D. H. Bull and his

41

wife and their large family that the walk bordering the lawn became widely known as the Nun's Walk.

I recall travelling to Harrow to interview the brother of the Rev L. A. Foyster and he showed me a photograph of the late Mrs H. D. E. Bull and spoke of at least one occasion when she saw the nun herself. When she told her husband, he recalled that it was the reputed anniversary of the nun's regular appearance and Mr Foyster was emphatic in stating that the Rev H. D. E. Bull knew all about the date on which the phantom was supposed to appear and their daughter Miss Ethel Bull, in a letter to me dated 22 September 1954 refers to her parents knowing all about the nun. This is important as some people assert that the appearance of the ghost nun on the path that became known as the Nun's Walk and the date on which she was supposed to appear each year dated from the 1900 appearance witnessed by the Bull sisters.

Curious happenings in the garden, recounted by Harry Bull, include the occasion when the family retriever suddenly started to howl and cower in fright; when the rector looked in the apparent direction of the dog's terrified gaze, he saw a man's legs visible through the lower part of tall and heavily-laden fruit bushes. He then saw the legs move and when clear of the bushes, Harry Bull saw that the figure was headless! Miss Ethel Bull well remembered this incident and talked to me about it. Another time her brother Harry saw the form of a little old man standing in the middle of the lawn with one arm pointing upwards and the other down; as the rector approached the figure vanished. Many years later Raymond Armes, life member of the Ghost Club Society and an experienced photographer, took a photograph that seemed to depict a similar figure.

The Rev Harry Bull claimed to see the phantom coach and horses several times and each time, as he watched, it disappeared. One night, as he was about to enter the rectory gate, he heard a great clatter of hooves and the rumbling of heavy wheels in the roadway behind him. As he stepped to one side he heard the sounds pass along the road but saw nothing to account for them. Some ten years later Herbert Mayes, chauffeur to a later rector of Borley, the Rev A. C. Henning, had an almost identical experience. He told me he was passing the rectory grounds on 16 March 1939 (less than three weeks after fire had gutted the building) when he heard the sound of approaching horses. He stood out of the way close to the hedge and shone a light in the direction of the sounds. The sound of galloping horses approached, passed him and died away in the distance – but he saw nothing to account for the sounds! Fourteen years later similar sounds were heard by Dr A. J. B. Robertson, a council member of the Society for Psychical Research, and four of his friends when they were paying a visit to the rectory site as one of a series that became known as the Cambridge Commission. Dr Robertson himself told me of the experience at a London meeting of the SPR.

During the course of Harry Price's initial visit in July 1929 to the haunted rectory he talked to many people who told him they had experienced inexplicable phenomena in the grounds of Borley Rectory. Several maidservants, including Mary Pearson (whom I talked with twenty-five years later) claimed to have seen the figure of the phantom nun on the Nun's Walk and a similar figure that disappeared near the bottom of the garden; others reported a 'shadowy figure' seen leaning over one of the drive gates – a shape that disappeared on investigation. One maid said she had seen the ghost coach-and-horses on the lawn and it disappeared into the hedge bordering the road travelling towards the church. In later years one of my investigators established that a road once ran beside the church where now there are fields so perhaps the phantom coach-and-horses was seen on the road that a real coach-and-horses had once taken.

One of the most remarkable reports of the appearance – or appearances – of the Borley nun is that related by a journeyman carpenter to Harry Price. Fred Cartwright lived at Sudbury and during the early autumn of 1927 he was working on some farm buildings between Borley and Clare. Each morning he would walk to his work, passing Borley Rectory on his way. The rectory was in fact empty at this time, the Rev Harry Bull having died in June 1927 and the Rev G. Eric Smith not yet having been inducted to the living and taken up residence, which he did in 1928. One day as he passed the deserted rectory when it was barely light, Cartwright saw a Sister of Mercy standing by the gatepost. She looked absolutely solid and normal but stood very still as though she was waiting for someone. During the next few days Cartwright saw nothing as he passed the rectory and then one morning he caught sight of her standing at exactly the same spot. He thought this rather peculiar and he looked hard at her as he passed. Again she appeared perfectly normal – except that her eyes were closed. He thought perhaps she had spent the night tending the sick and was resting; he continued on his way. Five days later he saw her again and again she was standing by the gatepost. He looked closely as he passed and thought she looked pale, tired and ill but otherwise perfectly normal; again her eyes were closed. This time, after he had walked on, he felt that something may be wrong and wondering whether he could help, he turned to offer assistance. But when he reached the gatepost, she was nowhere to be seen.

The fourth and last time Fred Cartwright saw the nun was a few days later, again at the same spot and at the same early hour when it was barely light. This time he decided to speak to her as he approached but when he was within a few steps of reaching her – she vanished. 'One moment she was there, the next she had gone', he said. He decided she must have gone into the rectory grounds and more than a little puzzled, he opened the gate and walked in. He walked the length of the drive, past the house, from one gate to the other, and he had a view of the entire lawn and garden; there was no sign of the figure he had seen. That night, when he got home, he spoke of his experiences and then, for the first time, heard some of the stories and traditions associated with Borley Rectory, including the phantom nun. He never saw the figure again, although he always looked as he passed empty Borley Rectory.

Thirty years later Dr Peter Hilton-Rowe, another life member of The Ghost Club Society, had a similar experience when he saw a black, nun-like figure with a sad look on her face walk quickly towards the south-east end of the rectory garden. He immediately examined the whole area but found no sign of a nun or anyone else. It is interesting to note that most, if not all, of those who claim to have seen the ghost nun at Borley remark on her 'looking as if she had been crying', having a 'drawn face', being 'pale-faced' or having 'looked sad'. Fragmentary human remains unearthed in the cellars at Borley Rectory including part of a skull and a jaw-bone were identified as probably belonging to a young woman of about thirty or younger and I discussed this fact with Leslie Godden, a West End dental surgeon who had examined the remains in 1945 and he said there was indisputable evidence of a deep-seated infection which would have resulted in a good deal of persistent pain. Could this have been the reason for the nun's sad face? The remains were buried by the Rev A. C. Henning in Liston churchyard.

During the Second World War an army sergeant attached to a searchlight battery at Belchamp Walter happened to pass the rectory site late one night on his way back to camp. Half way up the hill leading to the burnt-out shell of the rectory on one side of the road and the church on the other, he saw two lights coming towards him very fast. He thought it might be a private car but about a hundred yards from him the lights switched across the road and disappeared and Samuel Seal noticed a large dark shape following them . . . He thought the vehicle must have gone through the gates of the old rectory but when he reached the spot where the 'phantom manifestation' or whatever it was had vanished, he found the gate closed. I talked with Mr Seal and he was emphatic that something disappeared through the closed gate that night and he had been so intrigued that he had stopped and opened the gate and walked through. Inside, in the rectory garden, there was no sign of anything to account for what he had seen. Only later, when telling some of his friends what had happened, did he learn that the rectory and grounds were long said to be haunted.

Other unexplained happenings reported from the haunted garden at Borley Rectory were the experiences of Mr H. F. Russell, the manager of a well-known cable company who visited the site with his two sons, one a wing-commander and the other a squadron-leader, when Russell felt himself seized from behind and dashed to the ground where he landed in a pool of mud . . . there was no obvious cause or reason.

A number of instances of inexplicable stone-throwing was reported for years from the site of the haunted rectory garden. Three Polish Army Medical Corps officers, including their commanding officer, Lieutenant Nawrocki who had long been interested in scientific psychical research, reported on no less than six occasions stones being thrown at them and three days later a pebble struck Miss Mary George, a friend of Robert Aickman (with whom I discussed the mysteries of Borley on many occasions); Aickman, a prize-winning writer and founder of Inland Waterways

Association, was a shrewd and careful observer who was absolutely certain that Borley rectory had a haunted garden.

Over the succeeding years inexplicable stone-throwing was reported by scores of people, residents, visitors, clergymen, policemen and the occasional psychical researcher. As far as human testimony can prove anything, stones have been thrown by preternatural means in the garden at Borley, not to mention the numerous occasions when similar instances occurred inside the rectory itself.

Footsteps, the commonest of all reported activity in haunted houses – and in haunted gardens – was also reported at Borley. When the rectory was occupied there were many such reports; when it stood empty there were more and in fact just about everyone who lived at the rectory or after the fire, at the cottage, reported unexplained footsteps in the garden and indeed my friend of many years, Tom Brown (life member of the Ghost Club Society) and I heard them ourselves during a visit back in 1947. In an article published in *The Psychic Review* (volume XI number 4) dated March 1949 I stated: 'All that now remains of the rectory are the foundations and the cellars, and these are being altered by the present owner into an attractive sunken garden. But still the site is haunted. Twice during the night we spent in the grounds my associate and I heard footsteps from the direction of the Nun's Walk. We investigated on both occasions immediately and searched thoroughly. We were satisfied the footsteps were not of human origin.'

An electrical engineer, Mr Arthur Medcraft of Goodmayes, Essex visited Borley on many occasions, nearly always experiencing nothing out of the ordinary but on one visit, during the month of July 1943, when the rectory shell was deserted, he heard distinct footsteps following him as he approached the blackened building. He turned round but there was nothing to account for the sounds and they ceased as he turned. When he resumed walking the following footsteps sounded again, more slowly this time. Still walking Arthur Medcraft turned his head suddenly but there was nothing behind him.

When the ruins had been totally demolished and the bricks sold Captain Russell and his family bought the place and lived for a while in the cottage. Steuart F. C. Kiernander, another Ghost Club Society member whom I knew for more than thirty years, visited Borley at this period and talked with one of Captain Russell's daughters who told him she had seen figures in the garden she could not account for and she and her father had heard footsteps and other strange sounds that they could not explain.

Some visitors to the site have discovered that their photographic equipment has behaved oddly or simply refused to function at all. Dr Peter Hilton-Rowe went to Borley in 1947 to take some photographs for Harry Price and quickly found that his exposure meter simply would not work while he was in the old rectory garden although it worked perfectly when he left the rectory garden. He returned to the haunted garden but the same thing happened, although while away from the site the meter worked perfectly; in the churchyard, on the roadway and in the field opposite; he gave it a rest and then returned to the garden but it was no good, he could not get the meter to work there. He had never had this trouble before nor did he afterwards. Similar seemingly inexplicable interference with apparatus took place during one BBC broadcast. During interviewing in the garden a series of short, sharp raps were heard (and recorded) apparently emanating from the old cellars; raps that ceased and began again as requested by Peter Eton from the BBC who himself told me of this really mysterious incident when he was recording a broadcast.

Unexplained odours, smells and scents have been reported from the garden: the localised smell of lavender in a spot where there was no lavender; the strong smell of cooking (this on at least six occasions over a period of three years) often at dead of night; a most unpleasant odour, again very localised but totally inexplicable; and the strong smell of incense.

Among the unexplained sounds heard in that garden at Borley have been the sound of a dog panting and this sound seemed to follow the witness as she walked along the Nun's Walk, although nothing was visible. It sounded so close she could not believe that there was no dog there but she and her companion confirmed to me that there was certainly no dog, or at least no visible dog.

What may have been something similar, a sound so definite and realistic that the hearer almost disbelieved the evidence of his or her own ears, was heard by Mrs Cathy Turner. She told me that one summer day when her husband was busy she took a deckchair and a book and went and sat on the lawn James had planted in the middle of the garden. After a while she heard footsteps approaching and she waited to be disturbed but no one appeared. She looked round but there was no one in sight. Returning to her book, she had hardly found her place when she heard footsteps again and this time she listened very carefully and they sounded as though they were on solid wooden flooring but of course there was nothing but grass all round her. This time she did not look round but simply waited and listened and the footsteps seemed to approach her, pass at her side, turn in front of her and then retrace their tracks behind her, gradually fading and ceasing.

A couple of weeks later the same experience was repeated in the same spot. Where Cathy sat the old rectory had once stood and it was almost as though someone was walking again through the rooms of the vanished rectory. In the three years that James and Cathy Turner lived in the cottage at Borley this was her most memorable experience and one she would always remember, Cathy herself told me on several occasions. Some years later, a succeeding owner of the rectory site heard distinct footsteps on open ground in the garden in broad daylight. He had a clear view of the spot at the time and it was totally deserted.

James Turner, a delightful poet, author and broadcaster, had his own story to tell of inexplicable happenings in the garden at Borley. Soon after they took up residence James began to clear the overgrown brambles and rubbish from the Nun's Walk. At the end of May and the beginning of June, working mostly in the evenings with a sickle, he began to bring some order back to the historic garden and practically every evening, as he broke through the undergrowth into the old orchard, the sound of laughter and chattering came clearly to him, although no words were distinguishable. The voices came from the direction of the vanished rectory and sometimes James would lay down his sickle and listen but, as he did this, the sounds invariably died away. Sometimes he would call Cathy and, as her husband worked, clearing the old path that had long been hidden, she would also hear the voices, but as soon as he stopped working the voices stopped too. Once the sounds so tantalised him that he dashed through the brambles to try and catch some words but the voices, as James put it to me, 'happy and laughing, fled before me'. He never had any fear of the voices, only delight at experiencing the unexplained. When the work was completed and the path cleared, they never heard the voices again.

A lay investigator who became very interested in the Borley story for a while, Mr C. Groom-Hollingsworth, visited Borley on a number of occasions, sometimes accompanied by his friends Mr F. Cornell and Mr R. Potter and they too heard – and recorded – the sounds of animated conversation near the Nuns Walk when no living person was near but again no actual words were distinguishable.

Once Connell and Potter reported seeing the figure of a nun on the Nun's Walk, wearing clothing of a light grey or blue colour and at the time they thought they had obtained a moving picture of the apparition but there was nothing on the resulting film.

Among other witnesses who claimed to see the figure of a nun on the Nun's Walk at Borley, usually when the place was empty and deserted, are the Rev A. C. Henning; the local and previously sceptical Dr Abernethy; Terrence Bacon; Mr Williams; Gerard Kelman; Miss Jean Conolly and her sister Miss Margaret Conolly and there are many more but lists of names become onerous; suffice to say that from the time it was built in 1863, for more than a hundred years, people from all walks of life, of all ages and of every persuasion imaginable, have persistently reported apparently inexplicable happenings – and especially the figure of a nun – in what was once the haunted garden of Borley Rectory, long known as 'the most haunted house in England'.

BRAMSHILL HOUSE
Near Hartley Wintney, Hampshire

Even the police have had arresting experiences at Bramshill House, the police training college near Hartley Wintney in Hampshire – indeed it has long been widely known as 'Hampshire's most haunted house'. And it is not only the house that is haunted; there, if ever there was one, is a really haunted garden.

Bramshill House itself is of great antiquity and considerable interest. It is mentioned in the Domesday Book in the eleventh century and there was a substantial house on the site of the present mansion in the fourteenth century. The estate was bought by Edward, Lord Zouche of Harringworth in 1605 and he at once set about building his new house on the foundations of the old one; incorporating much of the original fabric and taking seven years, it was completed in 1612. Part of the original cellars and the fourteenth century gateway exist to this day.

Over the years a disastrous fire and various construction and improvement have narrowed the original courtyard but in spite of such alterations the fine mansion still retains much of the original façade and it is a very fine example of late Renaissance architecture. Bramshill was owned by the Cope family from 1699 to 1935 when it was bought by Lord Brocket who sold it to the Crown in 1953. From the beginning of 1954 it was used as a wing of the police college situated near Coventry; in 1960 the police staff college moved in its entirety to Bramshill.

Although they are more reluctant in the present climate to encourage visits and investigations – in 1993 they told our investigations officer that they felt security would be a problem (even in Britain's foremost police college!) – I am fortunate in having been there on a number of occasions, on my own, with my wife, accompanied by my grandson Toby, in the company of historian Dorothea St Hill Bourne and I have spent several nights there, in the company of fellow-members of The Ghost Club Society, with a *Sunday Times* representative and with Dr Sidney Scott, the acknowledged authority on Joan of Arc.

It is widely believed that Lord Zouche intended the house as a gift for King James I's eldest son, Henry, Prince of Wales, but after the tragic, sudden and mysterious death of the Prince (an enduring suspicion is that he was poisoned), Lord Zouche himself lived at what is generally considered to be one of the most beautiful houses of the period and he remained there until his death in 1625.

Dorothea St Hill Bourne knew Lieutenant-Colonel the Hon E. Gerald French DSO, who in turn had known Bramshill in the time of the thirteenth baronet Sir Anthony Cope, from whom he had heard the most famous ghost story associated with Bramshill; the story of the old oaken chest immortalised by Haynes Bailey in his 1828 poem, 'The Mistletoe Bough'. Whether the great carved chest, admittedly labelled 'The Bride's Chest', has anything to do with the Grey Lady or any of the other ghosts that undoubtedly walk at Bramshill may be open to question but former owner Lord Brocket had no doubt; he told me he truly believed the gruesome event had indeed taken place at Bramshill and he was quite determined that whoever bought the house must buy the Mistletoe Bough Chest. 'This house is the chest's spiritual home,' he said, and today the chest stands in the entrance hall of Bramshill House. Once, he told me, a descendant of the Cope family wrote to him, claiming the chest as the property of the Cope family and adding, 'If your heart is in the right place, you will send me back my chest' and Lord Brocket replied with characteristic wit: 'My heart is in the right place – it is in my chest!'

The story – with variations – concerns the wedding day of the beautiful daughter of the family one Christmas Eve and the house was decked with holly and the bride carried a sprig of mistletoe. After the ceremony and wedding breakfast the bride challenged her new husband and all the guests to find her in a game of hide-and-seek and she sped off to hide. The bridegroom, family and friends are said to have spent hours searching high and low with growing concern – but they did not find the bride. A new day dawned and the search went on and still no sign of the bride. She had wandered off into a little-used wing of the house and there chanced upon a huge chest which she thought would provide an ideal hiding place. Jumping in, she pulled the lid down and waited, not knowing that the click as the lid closed meant that the chest was for all practical purposes locked fast, and could only be opened from outside. In fact it was several days before the chest was examined and the bride's body found.

So distressed were the family that they went to France and stayed there for two years. On their return to Bramshill the entire wing where their daughter's body had been discovered, was demolished. Only the chest itself was preserved. During research at Bramshill, with the helpful assistance of the librarian there, I came to the conclusion that, while it was difficult to establish that the grim episode had in fact taken place (for there did not appear to be any marriage of a daughter of the house at Christmas), it was a fact that at one time the family had suddenly gone abroad, had

lived there for several years, and on their return a complete wing of the house had been demolished. So the story of the Mistletoe Bride must remain just one more of the intriguing mysteries at Bramshill. It is a mystery that, like all good mysteries, deepens as one seeks to fathom it. It has to be said too that several other old houses claim exactly the same story! What is not in doubt is that the figure of a beautiful girl, dressed in a white bridal gown and carrying a sprig of mistletoe has been seen many times in this lovely old house, especially in the vicinity of the present library.

Fred Cook spent nearly forty years helping to look after this brooding mansion and from time to time various employees would tell him of a personal encounter with the phantom girl or 'Lady in White' but Fred did not believe in ghosts at that time and used to tell the puzzled ghost-seer that it must have been a trick of the light. Then a footman came down one morning and said a lovely young lady had walked through his bedroom in the middle of the night and a few mornings later he said the experience had been repeated and this time when he saw her he jumped out of bed and put his arms around her, but as he did so she dissolved into thin air, leaving a strong flowery scent behind her.

This intrigued Fred Cook as many people had already told him that in certain rooms they had encountered the strong scent of flowers as they entered and he found that these were always the same rooms, although the people who reported the matter to him were unaware of previous reports relating to those rooms.

Then one evening Fred Cook saw the mysterious lady for himself. He had made a tour of the house at dusk, accompanied by his big labrador dog. 'I opened the door of the Long Gallery,' he told me. 'And there, staring at me, was this lady. If I was mistaken my dog wasn't. She gave a howl of terror and fell over backwards, then ran for home as fast as she could – and I wasn't far behind her!' After a few moments to collect his thoughts Fred remembered his responsibilities and went back to the Long Gallery, leaving his dog, shivering with terror, in front of the fire at home. He opened the big door quietly and peered cautiously into the haunted, historic, atmosphere-laden Long Gallery. It was completely devoid of anything as far as he could see but there lingered everywhere in the enormous room the unmistakable smell of flowers – lilies possibly; Fred Cook never forgot that experience of seeing a ghostly form and experiencing the flower scent that he had been told about so often. Nor was he alone in seeing a mysterious ghost at Bramshill.

After the Second World War the Rumanian royal family lived at Bramshill for a time and the King and Queen and the two royal children all claimed to see the ghost. I recall being shown the apparently comfortable room once occupied by the royal children. The unexplained figure of a young woman in a white dress and carrying a sprig of mistletoe was reported to disturb the children so frequently by passing silently through the room at night that both the King and the Queen asked Fred Cook to let the children occupy another room. No sooner had the children been given another room than the Queen asked Fred the name of the beautiful young lady staying at Bramshill. 'There isn't one,' replied Fred Cook, but the Queen insisted that there was. 'She was sitting in the King's chair, facing the television. When I looked again she had gone. I neither heard nor saw her come or go.' On another occasion the King asked about the young lady in the white dress he had encountered who disappeared in puzzling circumstances.

Indeed most of the rooms and passages, winding stairways and extensive gardens at Bramshill seem to be haunted. There is the ghost of a little old man with a long beard who is often seen at certain windows in the hall, looking in from the garden; there is the Fleur-de-Lys Room (so-called from its decoration) where some visitors report the presence of an invisible child – almost as soon as they become aware of a small hand nestling its way into theirs, the sensation disappears but a considerable number of people have reported the experience, not knowing of course that other people had reported a similar experience. There is an unoccupied room where the sound of a crying child has been heard; a room that has an icy atmosphere although centrally heated; another room where a sudden whistling wind invades its draught-proof confines; a corridor where a male ghost in seventeenth-century attire walks; and a modern phantom form of a young man walks through the reception area and disappears into a wall. On more than one occasion the Chapel Drawing Room has been found seemingly crowded with people in period costume, floating a foot or so above the level of the existing floor – and a moment later the room is deserted. Once this remarkable phenomenon was witnessed by three of the administrative staff and I talked with several staff members who had experienced the 'lovely flower smell' more than once, in quite inexplicable circumstances. A security guard felt a sudden gust of cold air and looking round saw the shadowy figure of a lady in a white robe; Mrs Denzil Cope awoke one morning to see a sad-looking woman with golden hair leaning over her bed and the same figure was seen on a number of occasions by other residents; once a senior police officer encountered a 'lovely lady with teardrops on her cheeks and her dark eyes had a kind of dead look in them' – she passed him without a sound and he watched as she disappeared into a solid wall; at the time he had no idea that Bramshill was haunted. And so the evidence goes on and on and it would be good to carry out a full investigation at Bramshill, but if we did so I would like to concentrate on specific parts of the garden.

One event that took place in the garden could well have contributed to the atmosphere conducive to ghosts. During the course of a visit to Bramshill the Most Reverend George Abbot, Archbishop of Canterbury, went out to shoot deer with a crossbow but shot instead a keeper on the estate. The barbed arrow pierced the keeper's arm, severing an artery, and within an hour the man was dead. Overcome with remorse and affected by the public outcry that followed the accident, the Archbishop was suspended from his office and retired into seclusion to await the verdict of an ecclesiastical enquiry. Ultimately the Archbishop was restored to his clerical position but it is said that he rarely smiled again and certainly he did all he could to provide for the widow of the unfortunate keeper. It transpired that Lord Zouche had warned the keeper to stand well clear of His Grace, whose shooting was known to be erratic. Sudden death amid tragic circumstances has been known to provide the conditions necessary to spark off psychic activity and there have been many such incidents in the history of Bramshill. Even the vision of a beautiful young woman dressed in a flowing white gown that has been witnessed on many occasions running along the corridors or passing through rooms at Bramshill has also long been reported to sometimes be seen walking in the garden.

There is a little bridge that carries the long drive from the Tudor gatehouse over a stream and my friend Dorothea St Hill Bourne learned from one of the first commandants at Bramshill that one day he and a fellow police officer both saw a figure standing on the bridge. The whole length of the mile-long drive was in view from the terrace where the two men were standing. The police officer set off to warn the intruder that whoever it was was trespassing but it was a very puzzled and disgruntled policeman who returned, for when he had reached the bridge no one was anywhere in sight, nor was there any nearby cover where anyone could have hidden. It was just one of many strange happenings in the gardens at Bramshill.

For years horses shied when passing a stretch of water known as the Pale Pond, the haunt of a mysterious Grey Lady always thought to be one of the Cope family for it is a ghost that was often seen when the Copes lived at Bramshill but not reported previously. Little Penelope Cope (who wrote a book about Bramshill when she was only twelve years of age) was still in her pushchair when her nurse and her mother were not infrequently puzzled when the little girl began to talk about a 'green man' whom she said she often saw about the house and park, generally near water: the lake, a pond, a large puddle or even the child's bath. Asked to describe anything unusual or disturbing about the figure, the child would reply, 'like Daddy – but no legs'.

Penelope's mother, Mrs Denzil Cope, had been assured on her marriage that she could discount the Bramshill ghost stories but now she was not so sure, especially when she discovered that an eccentric Cope ancestor had a passion for the colour green. He used to dress continually in green, from head to foot, down to the smallest detail, even carrying a green whip and wearing green gloves; he had the interior of his house and the furniture painted green and he lived on green fruit and vegetables. Only his boots were black for he always wore the fashionable Hessions, unobtainable in green. Could this account for the child's description? A figure seen at some distance dressed entirely in green but with black boots might well look as though it had no legs. This strange little man threw himself into the sea and to his death from the cliffs near Brighton in 1806 and one wonders whether the watery manner of his death accounts for his ghost's predilection for water. The lake near the mansion where the Green Man is said to appear most often is where, legend has it, the Black Prince was drowned.

After giving a lecture on 'Ghosts' at Grayshott Hall a titled member of my audience wrote to me from Blessington, Co. Wicklow as follows: '. . . I thoroughly enjoyed your talk at Grayshott which, alas, was only too short! I was particularly interested to hear you talking about Bramshill. I grew up at Hackwood not too far away – and knew Joan Penelope Cope and her young brother Antony. The former was an exact contemporary of mine and we became great friends. I often went to tea at Bramshill and she attended the dancing class at my home. I think she was about eleven or twelve when she wrote and illustrated the book all about Bramshill and its ghosts. It was very well written, and her publishers very wisely did not correct her spelling! She mentions the "Green Man" several times, and there was an illustration of Anthony aged about three years old, sitting in his bath and saying "Der's de Geen Man". As you mentioned, he was always seen near water; she also saw the Green Man frequently . . . I also remember her telling me in a very matter-of-fact way that often a beautiful young girl came and sat on the end of her bed: she had a very sad face, and there was a faint smell of flowers when she was in the room. Joan felt that she came to make sure that all was well. There may well be some connection with the Bride in the Chest? The Cope children lived in a little world of their own, and I know how miserable they were when Bramshill was sold. Someone asked Anthony if he missed living there and he replied, "Very much, but most of all we miss our ghosts – they must be very lonely without us" . . . Certainly bad luck seemed to dog the Copes after they left their home.

Anthony threw himself out of a train when he was a young man. Joan married Sir Duncan Grant who shot himself in a car park in Scotland. Joan moved to Dublin after his death, with her five children from the marriage. I did see her several times but then she became terminally ill with Alzheimer's Disease and died last year . . .'

A famous appearance of what would appear to be an ancestral ghost was the dramatic appearance late one evening in front of Penelope's great-grandfather, Sir William Cope, and several members of his family. Practically the whole household was on the terrace when suddenly they all saw the white-robed figure of a woman leaning over the balustrade at the far end of the terrace. Thinking that one of the housemaids must be sleep-walking in her nightdress, Sir William sent the butler to deal with the situation. As the butler advanced down the terrace, he and the rest of the assembled company saw the white-robed figure leap over the balustrade and disappear. No explanation was ever found for this incident.

There is one spot in the garden at Bramshill where some people have felt abject terror. Fred Cook, that long-time employee at the historic mansion, had the distinct impression that he was being followed as he approached the place, time after time, and the awful feeling of absolute terror increased until he was past the spot, when it gradually diminished. Deciding that discretion was the better part of valour, Fred took to avoiding the place altogether and then one day he mentioned the matter to a lady who had lived thereabouts for years. 'You are not the only one to have known the feeling of terror there,' she said. 'Every evening I used to take my dogs for a walk in that direction. At the exact spot you describe I always felt completely overcome by a mortal fear. I remember once it was dusk on a lovely summer day but I felt a sense of utter panic and my dogs, who would have stood by me against anything that was made of flesh and blood, had gone running away from me. I found them cringing with fear, howling, and now I never go along that walk if I can help it.'

Other people, with no knowledge of anything unusual happening at Bramshill have had strange experiences. Mr T. Phipps of Tilehurst wrote to me saying he used to deliver goods to Bramshill in the course of his work and on one occasion he had completed his business and was driving his Bedford van away from Bramshill when, just past the security barrier opposite the lake, he stopped momentarily to sort out his invoices and to check on his next delivery. Suddenly he felt an icy chill (although the van had an extremely efficient heater) and the invoices and papers slipped out of the clipboard – seemingly an impossibility – and as the icy chill increased Mr Phipps managed to slam the van into gear and he pushed off quickly; and he made sure he never stopped at that place on subsequent visits.

The haunted gardens of Bramshill would almost certainly repay some quiet but exhaustive investigation by experienced psychical researchers for rarely do we find such an abundance of varied and well-authenticated psychic activity within the confines of such a beautiful, atmospheric and historic building.

Air Commodore Harold Shephard, Provost Marshall of the RAF, but once an uncomplicated police constable, dismissed the police college at Bramshill as 'a policeman's polytechnic' where the leadership was plodding and pedestrian. It cannot but be interesting that it was once owned and lived in by some of the highest in the land and the living residents made no difference to the reports of ghosts and ghostly happenings which seem always to have manifested there and still do so. Nor is it uninteresting to learn that another police training college, beautiful seventeenth-century Chantmarle Manor in Dorset, was well-known for its Grey Lady ghost when the manor was occupied by the police!

BRETFORTON MANOR
Bretforton, near Evesham, Worcestershire

The pleasant grounds of sixty-six room Bretforton Manor near Evesham in the very heart of England take on a sombre atmosphere during the hours of darkness; at least they did when I was there on an investigative visit some years ago. At the time the owner and occupier was Derek Chapman who described the house to me as 'such an interesting house with ghosts all over the place, but they all seem to be quite nice ghosts, not wicked ones at all. I suppose you might call it a happy haunting ground!'

The ghosts he and others saw in the garden included 'a figure in a bell-shaped cloak who glided into the trees and disappeared; and the figure of an old woman'. Derek Chapman believed all the ghosts were members of the Ashwin family who owned and lived at Bretforton Manor for 450 years. 'They even had their own cemetery in the grounds . . .' I was told. There is also supposed to be a phantom funeral procession, black plumed horses and all, that winds its way through the garden, en route to the church close by. From the haunted garden you descend ancient stone steps and there is the time-honoured Fleece Inn, a quaint old hostelry that was originally a farmhouse, believed to date back to the fourteenth century and one of the few inns owned by the National Trust. Inside on the stone floor there are 'witch marks' designed to keep away evil spirits and a reminder of the inn's medieval past, while among the antiques preserved there is a forty-eight-piece set of Stuart pewter. Nearby, ancient Byrd's Cottage has walls that lean at gravity-defying angles, and a carved face guards one of its doors. It is a quite remarkable area.

The manor itself, extensively renovated in 1871 by W. H. Ashwin, has a reception hall heavily carved in black oak, some of which is reputed to have been part of a chapel from a Spanish ship that was driven aground during the Spanish Armada debacle, with carvings dedicated to St Monica, a wife and mother who was made a saint in 387 AD.

Other features of the manor include the dining room with its fourteen-seater dining suite in oak and its walls two-thirds panelled in oak – a part of the 1871 restoration

– although it still retains the beautiful seventeenth-century black oak overmantel. There is a passageway leading to the Library, which contains a long half-panel of carved oak, also probably put there in 1871. The Library itself has a fine seventeenth-century carved, black oak overmantel and on the right-hand side there is an excellently preserved priest hole from Cromwellian days. There is also a banqueting hall with a huge open fireplace and ancient kitchens, interesting wine cellars, several eighteenth- and nineteenth-century iron fireplaces and remarkable nineteenth-century bathrooms. The official 'Brief Notes on Bretforton Manor', from which much of this information is taken, ends with four simple words: 'The house is haunted'.

The manor was in fact built by the Ashwin family soon after the dissolution of the monasteries by Henry VIII and it remained in the hands of that family until it passed to Derek Chapman in 1984. There has long been a persistent story that Queen Elizabeth stayed at the manor, and while this could well have happened there does not appear to be any concrete evidence for such a visit. One definite 'royal' visitor was the Duc d'Orléans who certainly stayed at Bretforton Manor together with his not inconsiderable retinue.

He readily agreed to an investigative visit and as he welcomed us to his wonderful home 'Squire' Chapman (as he was entitled to call himself) had a word for each of us and then showed us all round the house and garden and then we settled in the Banqueting Hall and he related something of the history of the house, its ghostly associations, and his personal experience of ghosts and ghostly happenings in the short time he had owned the manor.

We were interested to learn that six months previously Derek Chapman knew nothing of any alleged haunting at Bretforton Manor but since moving in he had seen apparitions or inexplicable shapes, found himself awake regularly between 3 and 4 a.m. whenever he occupied one of the front bedrooms, had discovered unexpected notes in passages, and had heard doors opening and closing themselves at least a dozen times. He had seen one apparition in the garden near the front door on three occasions and always just before midnight: a grey, indistinct, bell-like shape that he thought might be a cloaked figure, probably male and possibly a monk.

Just before three o'clock one afternoon he had encountered a man in an upstairs room; he appeared to be a butler or manservant of some kind – a figure that was there one minute and gone the next. Later he discovered that thirty years before a butler, known as Bertie, had died in that particular room.

When he first moved into Bretforton Manor, Derek Chapman had occupied a first-floor bedroom (which he had pointed out to us) and while sleeping there he had found himself inexplicably awake in the early hours almost every night. He had seen nothing and he had heard nothing but something had awakened him – and it was not anything very pleasant. His first thought on awakening each time was that he must get out of the room, but he was determined not to be told what to do in his own house and he stayed, but in the end whatever it was won and he never slept in that room afterwards and he would never allow anyone else to sleep there.

In several of the rooms and passageways, we were told, there were doors that opened and closed by themselves. This was not imagination. For security reasons he was particularly careful about closing all doors and windows at night but on many occasions he had heard the sound of a door opening and on going to investigate had found a door had indeed opened by itself. On other occasions he would hear a door he had purposely left open close, and again this was found to have happened. There did seem to be certain doors in the house that would not stay shut and others that would not stay open. On the other hand there were occasions when he distinctly heard the sound of a door opening or closing but he could discover nothing that could have caused the sounds, there having, apparently, been no movement of any doors in the house.

A room on the top floor, known as the Schoolroom, always seemed to light up of its own accord. This had been witnessed by people inside the house and also by other people outside the house in the garden. Six months previously a housekeeper had been put in this room but she had quickly asked to be moved to another room; she would give no reason – she just said she didn't like the Schoolroom. As far as is known she had no knowledge of the mysterious lights. Derek Chapman told us he had noticed that it was difficult to get dogs to enter that room; even the postmaster's great dane – who seemed to be familiar with every room in the house – couldn't be persuaded to go inside the Schoolroom.

In another bedroom, a guest, just the week before our visit, had seen the ghost of an elderly lady standing beside the bed. Here, ten years previously, but unknown to the visitor, a lady had been sleeping in the room and had awakened in the middle of the night to see an elderly lady leaning over the bed. When the visitor screamed, the figure vanished. Derek Chapman told us he felt this apparition was the same one he had encountered in other parts of the house and also in the garden.

There have been several violent deaths at Bretforton Manor over the years and for a considerable period of time a stain on a red carpet was said to mark the scene of a murder, a mark that for years, if not centuries, could not be eradicated. The carpet was eventually replaced. There was also the case of a servant girl, years ago, who had been found dead at the bottom of the stairs. At first it was thought she had fallen but subsequently it was established that she had been murdered by another servant who had fetched the police but at length was found to be guilty of the crime and paid the penalty.

The Library was haunted too and a male figure had been seen there by lots of witnesses. It was an unmoving figure that was always seen in exactly the same place. He seemed to be wearing 'old-fashioned' clothes; he seemed to be watching or waiting for something or someone, but who he was and why he waited no one now seemed to know. The Library had been largely unaltered for years.

There were many witnesses too for figures seen in the garden – male and female figures. Usually they seemed to be in a hurry and most of those who saw them did so out of the corner of their eyes and when they turned to fully face the figure or figures, they saw nothing. These figures had been seen in various parts of the garden, usually fairly close to the house, and at various times of the night and early morning. A number of objects had been moved in different parts of the house and also in the garden, and a few unidentified objects had mysteriously appeared, but unfortunately nothing of value!

During our visit a 'shadowy form' was seen on three separate occasions in the garden, by different people, but at the same place – and we established to our entire satisfaction that there was nothing of a normal nature, such as a tree, a bush, a reflection or anything of that nature that could have accounted for the form seen. Each time the mysterious form vanished inexplicably by the time other people appeared on the scene to corroborate the sighting. But three definite and independently reported sightings, by three different people, on three separate occasions, and all at the same place, and the observers having no knowledge of previous sightings – surely this must provide food for thought. There were also reported curious knocking and clicking sounds in the garden, not far from the front door on several occasions by different observers and, oddly enough, what would appear to be identical sounds were reportedly heard inside the house on different occasions outside the room we were using as our Base Room from where all activities of the night were controlled and recorded.

In the grounds there are, or were, the original stocks, dated 1360; a black-and-white thatched barn with a horse-drawn cider mill; an artificial lake; a clear running brook;

old stables and former paddocks and carriageways and here, among the paraphernalia of a past age, some of my friends felt a very strange atmosphere. One said she felt 'there was quite definitely a sense of transportation back in time in the vicinity of the stocks' and she couldn't help but feel that the whole house and the extensive garden were 'steeped in the past' and she has always felt since that 'those few hours spent at Bretforton Manor were not part of present-day life as we know it'.

Another friend present during this visit told me afterwards that 'wandering along the paths in the garden with the overlapping trees one felt the sense of an unhurried time long past, an unshakable Victorian empire perhaps . . .' He took many photographs in the garden using a high-speed film which did away with the necessity of using a flash. When he had all the films developed, the high-speed ones and the low-speed films he had used during the visit, he discovered all the photographs were disfigured with 'unusual markings' that might be described as 'ectoplasmic formations'. Had some of the 'spirits' decided to vacate haunted Bretforton Manor for the duration of our visit?

The overwhelming impression of practically everyone present on that memorable occasion was that earthbound spirits (for want of a better name) do wander abroad at Bretforton . . .

Buriton Manor
Buriton near Petersfield, Hampshire

Nestling under a fold in the south downs amid woods and away from the busy road carrying traffic from Petersfield to the coast lies the village of Buriton, a typical English village with its church, village pond and manor house.

Today Buriton Manor House is a mixture of old and very old, slumbering and preserving its several mysteries. It dates back many centuries. In 1719 it was bought by the grandfather of Edward Gibbon, who was a Member of Parliament, 'an old mansion in a state of decay'. In fact this timber-framed house is probably of fifteenth-century origin with a Georgian front and later additions. It occupies the site of the original manor, given to Queen Matilda by William the Conqueror in the eleventh century. Edward Gibbon, the historian (1737-1794), lived here after leaving Magdalen College, Oxford (which he heartily disliked) and during the next five years he spent freezing winters and hot summer days in the manor and on its manicured gardens reading for and preparing his monumental *Decline and Fall of the Roman Empire*, one of the foremost historical works of all time; although Gibbon viewed history as 'little more than the register of the crimes, follies and misfortunes of mankind'.

Perhaps it was sometime during those years – or even earlier – that a chambermaid or maidservant of some kind, or maybe a nanny, walked calmly out of the house, silently

crossing the garden and the expanse of lawn to reach the enormous barn that still stands facing the quiet, warm brick house – and there hanged herself.

Centuries later the sound of her echoing footsteps and the sight of her ghost solemnly traversing the grass in front of the house by moonlight – seemingly reconciled to the inevitable – has been reported times without number. In 1957 nearly all the English national daily newspapers stated that the then owner, Lieutenant-Colonel Algernon Bonham Carter, had applied to Petersfield Rural District Council, his local authority, for a reduction in the rates he had to pay on the manor; purely because the place was haunted! What is more, the council obviously accepted his claim and accordingly reduced the rates on Buriton Manor by £13 a year, a not inconsiderable sum in 1957. I have found – just as author Diana Norman did thirty years ago – that Petersfield District Council displays a curious reluctance to reveal details of the meeting at which the rates of the manor were reduced. But there is no disputing the newspaper reports of the day and it must be acknowledged that the house is – or certainly was at that time – so haunted that hard-headed local councillors accepted the fact without demur and acted accordingly, to the owner's evident satisfaction.

A later owner of Buriton Manor told me: 'There is no doubt that Lieutenant-Colonel Bonham Carter was very psychic and that the house was extremely haunted during his time. He certainly claimed to see the ghost chambermaid on more than one occasion'.

After the death of Lieutenant-Colonel Bonham Carter, Mr and Mrs Miller-Sterling took over the manor house. They certainly accepted that the newspaper reports were quite correct and that the manor house and garden were indeed haunted. Their son, when he was five years old, repeatedly talked of 'someone' entering his room at night and trying to take his pillow away as he slept: something a chambermaid or nanny might do perhaps to make the boy more comfortable. The Miller-Sterling boy was not the only child to report such a figure. The children of guests and friends staying at the house have casually mentioned a silent, watching figure who seemed to exude a feeling of protection and watching over their interest; certainly nothing in the least frightening. It is difficult to decide whether this figure, if she exists outside the imagination of the children concerned, is likely to be the girl with suicide on her mind, or someone else entirely. Children over the years seem to have been especially favoured by the sight of a smiling woman who watches them at play in the garden, in particular it seems when their play takes them anywhere near the haunted barn.

Other people, apart from residents and visitors, have reported hearing footsteps, both in the garden at the front of the house and from the direction of the underground passage that used to lead to the church just outside the grounds of the manor. The church building belonged to the manor until 1886. Both the footsteps heard walking along the reverberating underground passage in the direction of the church and those heard crossing the garden towards the barn have only been heard walking away from the manor; they have never been heard returning.

Some years ago my clairvoyant friend Tom Corbett visited Buriton Manor. He spent time in most of the rooms and passages, as I did quite recently, and he felt the presence of a friendly, warm-natured woman inside the manor; a woman who had the appearance of a nanny and he thought she was probably responsible for some of the reported disturbances at the manor. Oddly enough he felt no presence in the barn.

During one of my visits to Buriton Manor I spent some time alone in the enormous barn where the unhappy female servant hanged herself and I have to say I found the atmosphere unwelcoming and unpleasant; after half-an-hour it was so overwhelmingly sad and unhappy that I had to leave. I saw no ghost and I felt no presence but I can accept that something very sad happened there that has left behind traces of what took place, of the innermost feelings of the chief protagonist in the sad drama, and that some traces of all that can be picked up to this day.

One interesting facet of the haunting is that when the ghost of the distraught chambermaid or nanny has been seen crossing the garden towards the barn, she disappears into the solid side of the great building – and where she disappears there used to be an entrance to the barn long, long ago.

The evidence as to the identity of the main ghost, if any ghosts still walk at Buriton, is conflicting. Lieutenant-Colonel Bonham Carter's brother, Admiral Sir Stuart Bonham Carter, used to talk of the ghost being a 'dear little old lady'; various children have spoken of 'a smiling woman' and Tom Corbett sensed an 'elderly, warm-hearted woman', while Lieutenant-Colonel Algernon Bonham Carter, a recent occupant of the manor and numerous reports over the years suggest a chambermaid dressed in eighteenth-century attire, flitting across the lawn and disappearing into the barn.

On one visit, when the contents of the house were being sold, I talked with an inhabitant of nearby Petersfield who told me, when I casually asked whether he knew any legends associated with the house, that there was a very old story of a servant walking out of the house and committing suicide in the barn; a very old story, he insisted, long before Algernon Bonham Carter's time, and both he and his wife had actually seen the mysterious figure! At the time they erroneously thought it was someone practising a fancy dress and historical event to be held at the house. The figure appeared to be absolutely natural, solid and clear, but looking back afterwards they could not remember any sound whatever accompanying the sighting.

Wandering through Buriton Manor and its haunted gardens, back and front, it is not hard to recall that the house has seen a lot of history; it has absorbed a wealth of different people and personalities and over the long years the house has seen as much happiness and as much unhappiness as other historic houses where families have lived and loved and perhaps fought and even caused frustration and deep despair. The history of Buriton Manor is interwoven with stories of ghosts, insubstantial, passing figures who may perhaps be little more than shadows of themselves and their activities in days and nights long past.

Whatever the answers to the many mysteries of Buriton Manor, and perhaps there are at least two, maybe three, ghosts at Buriton, there appears to be no doubt that the beautiful, peaceful and tranquil garden at Buriton Manor is haunted.

CAMFIELD PLACE
Hatfield, Hertfordshire

Charming Camfield Place was long occupied by equally charming Dame Barbara Cartland, the celebrated romantic novelist, historian, playwright, political speaker, television personality, vitamin enthusiast and author of over 700 books who freely admits, 'I am very superstitious'. Beatrix Potter, whose grandfather built the place, was often frightened by ghosts there.

Over ninety years ago, walking along a country lane holding on to the perambulator containing her new baby brother, Barbara was helping their nanny on their daily walk. They stopped at a cottage where they were to leave some soup for a woman who was ill. While the nanny was on her errand of mercy the tiny Barbara walked across the lane and through some gates into a park full of colourful and scented flowers. As she stood looking at them the flowers seemed to come nearer to her, to get larger and larger. 'There was a strange vibration coming from them,' she was to write years later. 'I thought I could see them growing, living and breathing'. It was all quite

extraordinary and very exciting for the young child. 'I stood staring at those flowers all those years ago,' she told me, 'and I knew they were as alive as I was.' Suddenly the voice of her nanny broke into her reverie. 'Barbara – what are you doing? Come here at once . . .' The spell was broken but the memory and the significance of what she had seen and experienced lingered on.

In fact the life of Barbara Cartland has been peppered with curious and enlightening experiences. In Worcestershire in 1910 she sometimes glimpsed a fairy among the flowers. 'I could see her out of the corner of my eye,' she said, 'but when I turned my head she was gone.' Two years later, again in Worcestershire, she experienced the sensation of a tree breathing: 'Sometimes when I was alone in the garden I would put my ear against the trunk of a tree and I could hear it breathing and living. Everything has life in it like the life in me' she wrote in her diary, and two years later in Bath: 'I was in the bedroom thinking of my mother when on the wall in front of me I saw the huge outline of an angel. His head nearly touched the ceiling and his feet were only a few inches off the floor. He was outlined in light, like a drawing and only his wings had any substance. He did not move and his face, which was very beautiful, was turned sideways. I knelt and looked at him in amazement for several seconds, then he slowly faded.' Many years later, in the Sistine Chapel in Rome, Barbara Cartland saw a similar angel, the same magnificant lines and the same noble head, in a drawing by Michelangelo.

In her early teens Barbara Cartland lived at Nailsea Court in Somerset and, as she stated at the time, 'I am living in a ghost house. There is always someone going up the stairs ahead of me or coming up behind me; yet they cannot be seen. The house was very old and filled with the panelling and furniture of Judge Jeffreys – the Hanging Judge. Had his bitterness and cruelty survived all these years, I wondered. I was never alone. One night I heard footsteps dragging their way upstairs, and the tick of the

66

clock like the beat of a heart sounded and resounded in my ears. I was really terrified and prayed desperately. The footsteps stopped when they reached my door. Next day I learned that a cavalier who had been wounded by the Roundheads came back to the house to die.'

While living in Somerset Barbara Cartland frequently visited the old church where she had been confirmed. A beautiful manor house, built in the time of Charles I, but now locked and deserted, stood beside the church; its windows boarded up, the doors locked. Sometimes with friends Barbara tried to get in but they never succeeded. A local story said the family who lived at the manor house for centuries were Roman Catholics and that the house was haunted by an evil monk who became so troublesome that a cardinal was asked to exorcise the ghost.

Having performed the Service of Exorcism the cardinal said all was now well and he would sleep in the room himself. He awoke in the middle of the night to see the figure of a monk standing beside the bed. Before he could do anything the monk struck him and he knew no more.

He was ill for a long time, so ran the story, and when he recovered he said the family must leave the house and it should not be inhabited by anyone but allowed to fall into disrepair and eventually crumble to dust.

The church, Barbara said, was even older than the house and with the passing of the centuries it had sunk and now one walks down several steps to the aisle. There was a smell of age and dust and it was very dark; the stained glass windows were old and dirty and there were dark corners and strange shadows everywhere. That day as she walked in, the only other people present were the parson, a server and two very old women, yet Barbara knew that there were many more people in the church although they were not visible. 'I could feel them behind me, I could even hear them breathing,' she said, 'and if they were dead they were still tied to the earth. It was strange, eerie yet fascinating, and although there were other churches I could have attended, I used to go back, Sunday after Sunday, to the one where those who had lived in the haunted house worshipped for centuries and, who knows, perhaps they were the ghosts I frequently sensed in that old, old church.'

As early as 1926 Barbara Cartland was writing in her daybook: 'Ghosts, in many cases, are photographs. A violent crime is committed, the vibrations of murderer and victim are so strong that they charge the atmosphere with a permanent photograph of what has occurred. Sometimes certain weather conditions are required to develop the negative clearly for ordinary eyesight, sometimes only mediumistic and clairvoyant people, whose sensibilities are peculiarly sympathetic, can perceive what has once taken place. But the photograph is there all the time and, so far as we know, forever. What people call evil spirits are often the result of a strong personality pouring out into the air vibrations of life from themselves. A person with an intensely vital and strong character emits from himself strong vibrations directed with concentrated will power'.

One evening when she was motoring in the dark along a country road with a man who was a very good driver, she suddenly screamed 'Stop! Look out!' and she put her hands over her eyes. The driver calmly asked her what was wrong and continued to drive along the road. She told him she had quite clearly seen him drive into a flock of sheep! A little further on they stopped for a meal and at the hotel they learned that three years previously a car had driven into a flock of sheep at that very spot!

In 1935 in Vienna – which she loved – Barbara Cartland encountered a phantom cardinal in the cathedral there, the Stephansdom, which had the 'most moving atmosphere' she ever encountered anywhere. Sitting there watching all sorts and conditions of people come to pray before an allegedly 'miraculous' picture, the light from many candles flickering on the massive gold chandeliers hanging from the carved and painted roof, she saw the ghostly cardinal clearly outlined against the dark stone and she could even see his features and the expression on his face, which seemed to be deeply lined with suffering yet at the same time she saw in the expression a serenity and compassion as of faith transcending all the cruelties and stupidities of mankind. The figure, she told me, remained motionless for a long while before fading into nothingness.

In 1957 Barbara Cartland wrote: 'When I came to Camfield, I had the house blessed in case there might be a ghost in it. After my experiences in Somerset I disliked ghosts. But what is extraordinary is that now we have the ghost of one of our dogs who had been "put to sleep". My maid, who has always been psychic, has seen the dog two or three times in the hall, and I have seen it twice. Once it was lying under the table, and because I was carrying a big vase of flowers I pushed it with my foot saying: "Do get out of the way!" thinking it was Murray – one of the other spaniels. I touched nothing!

'At one time the ghost dog was so fierce that whenever Murray tried to eat his dinner in the dining-room he would give a shriek as if he had been bitten, and then back away from his dish snarling as if another dog was trying to take it from him. We have grown quite used to the ghost. It doesn't worry us, it was one of our own dogs, and it has all been written up in The Stately Ghosts of England. Tom Corbett, the Irish clairvoyant, came down and talked to me about it. He had been to Longleat, Littlecote, Salisbury Hall, and innumerable other stately homes where there were all sorts of remarkable ghosts with heads under arms, and he was obviously not very impressed with my poor little dog ghost. But when he left he said to me: "Have you got a son?" "Yes," I replied. "Does he drive a car?" I nodded and Tom Corbett said: "Tell him to be very careful for the next two or three days."

'It was really rather a wicked thing to say and I was terrified because my son, Glen, was on the Continent motoring with his cousin. I managed to reach him by telephone in Brussels. "Please darling, be careful," I pleaded. "Don't fuss, Mummy!" It was the reply of sons to anxious mothers all through the ages.

'The next night I was awoken about three o'clock in the morning by the noise of police cars beneath my bedroom window. I put my head out and asked what was happening. "There has been an accident to one of Mr McCorquodale's cars," I was told. What had really happened was that a young manservant, returning from a night out after drinking a lot with some friends, missed his way when the road curved and drove straight into a ditch. He turned the car over, missing a telegraph post by inches, and although he had only a few scratches the car was a total wreck.'

When I visited Camfield Place for the first time delightful Barbara Cartland – whom I had met years before at a book launching and we had corresponded from time to time – told me that the ghost dog had also been seen in the charming garden. 'My daughter-in-law saw it the other day,' Dame Barbara told me. 'A few years ago I had a pale brown spaniel called Jimmy. He became ill and I had to have him put down. Now he appears all the time; my staff have seen him, I have seen him, my family have seen him. I don't mind – he's my dog after all.'

I remember looking carefully around what was, in more ways than one, a haunted garden. Here had walked the wraith of a much-loved dog, seen by a lot of people who invariably took what they saw for a real dog. Here also had walked superstitious Donald Campbell, Lord and Lady Dowding, Tom Corbett and other individual personalities whom I also had known and talked with. What a wonderful place this was; what a wonderful person Dame Barbara Cartland was; and what a wonderful haunted garden this was here in a delightful corner of wonderful Hertfordshire.

N.B. Dame Barbara Cartland died 21 May 2000, two months before her 99th birthday.

CHARLECOTE PARK
Charlecote, Warwickshire

The best-known ghost at Charlecote Park is confined to the garden. A sad little ghost, the apparition of a young girl who trips lightly to the willow-shaded water and is quickly submerged. She is generally thought to be a suicide re-enacting her death by drowning, but who is she and why did she do it?

Some fifteen years ago I talked at length with Lady Fairfax-Lucy of Charlecote Park and gleaned a wealth of information about Charlecote and its ghosts, for Lady Fairfax-Lucy had personal experience of most of them.

This fine house was built on the traditional E plan in the 1500s by yellow-bearded Sir Thomas Lucy whose family had lived at Charlecote since the twelfth-century and it was before this same Sir Thomas Lucy that a certain Mister William Shakespeare is said to have been arraigned in the Great Hall after he was caught on a poaching expedition in the park which is still one of the finest parks in the Midlands. It is more than likely that at this time, to avoid legal proceedings, Shakespeare went to London where we next find him as an actor-dramatist. It seems he took revenge on Sir Thomas Lucy by ridiculing him as Mister Justice Shallow in *The Merry Wives of Windsor*.

It could be that Shakespeare used his knowledge of Charlecote in some of his other plays, for up to the turn of the twentieth-century the place was known as a resort of witches, one of whom, called Diana, rode a buck, and the particular coven that was active at Charlecote was credited with the ability to turn people into cattle. The park, laid out by 'Capability' Brown, still contains the descendants of the famous 'Shakespeare' herd of fallow deer and a flock of Spanish sheep of rare breed whose ancestors were brought here by a Lucy some 200 years ago. Sir Thomas Lucy entertained here Queen Elizabeth I for breakfast one day in 1576 when she was on her way to Kenilworth to see her favourite, Robert Dudley, Earl of Leicester. The house itself has been considerably altered inside and outside since Elizabethan days but the impressive gatehouse in front of the main house is exactly as Shakespeare and Queen Elizabeth I would have known it. A contemporary picture of Queen Elizabeth I is among the interesting portraits in the house.

Some say that when Shakespeare was caught red-handed at his midnight poaching, he was held prisoner for the rest of the night in the Great Hall, either 'held over' for interrogation or perhaps as a punishment. It has been suggested that Shakespeare retaliated immediately by writing a rude poem about Sir Thomas and affixing it to the gates for all to see, an act that so infuriated the owner-knight that Shakespeare could well have decided it prudent to hasten to London and 'disappear' for a time. Whatever the truth of the matter Shakespeare at Charlecote seems to be one of the comparatively few authenticated records of his life, other than his marriage and family, some of the plays attributed to him and his death.

Lady Fairfax-Lucy was in no doubt about Charlecote having its haunted apartments and garden and she told me, 'Our wing is virtually impregnated with a sense of the past; that is with the three generations who lived in it since it was built in the 1830s. The Green Room is in the original part of the old house and had a door opening on to the Minstrels' Gallery (taken down in the 1870s) above the Great Hall, and still there is a small room off it. I have myself been conscious of a pressure of people and an unidentifiable hubbub of voices when alone in the room. My daughter slept in the Green Room and confirmed this – she was awakened in the middle of the night to find herself in the middle of a crowd of people milling round her. But at the same time I have to say that other people have slept in the Green Room and experienced nothing untoward'. But, as Lady Fairfax-Lucy so rightly said: 'Ghosts are not to be commanded or regulated and, in my experience, appear to the most unlikely people at the most unlikely times.'

In answer to further questions about Charlecote's ghosts, Lady Fairfax-Lucy explained that this Green Room, a bedroom in the south wing, long reputed to be haunted, was then being used continually by members of the Lucy family. The confused noise of raised voices in the little room, once used by the musicians, had been heard by many people, including Lady Fairfax-Lucy herself, and it was usually described as sounding as though an argument was taking place, accompanied by some violence. Lady Fairfax-Lucy also told me about a trusted old servant who had been with the family for sixty years, who always maintained that the garden had two ghosts, the mysterious girl and a footman who also drowned himself and was 'sometimes seen: a dark figure standing by the waterfall . . .'

The identity of the shadowy figure of the ghostly girl is a long-standing mystery that may have its origin in far-off days when some members of the Lucy family were no better than they should have been and in particular one historical incident may be significant.

George, Duke of Northumberland, had become enamoured of pretty Catherine Lucy, widow of Captain Lucy of the Royal Horse Guards, but she insisted on matrimony. Within a year he had grown tired of her and he and his brother (who was a young man who welcomed all kinds of adventures) put their heads together and decided to kidnap Catherine and deposit her in a convent on the Continent.

These two, both illegitimate sons of Charles II by Barbara Castlemaine, managed successfully to inveigle Catherine aboard a ship, and in due course took her to a convent in Ghent where they also succeeded in persuading the Mother Superior to certify that Catherine had entered the convent voluntarily. In high glee at the outcome of their plan the brothers returned to England, but Catherine was a young woman with determination and spirit and she proved to be more than a match for the sly schemers. She escaped from the convent, made her way to London and sought out her husband. Threatened with scandal, Northumberland came to terms, but one wonders what kind of life and how much happiness Catherine enjoyed thereafter?

Could she or some other unlucky Lucy be the ghost? The ethereal figure of a girl has repeatedly been seen running down to the water and there disappearing, making no disturbance to the surface as the form sinks and is submerged. Could Shakespeare have seen this ghost himself? There is, after all, a persistent legend that this is the place where he was inspired to write his lines on Ophelia's death. Some people even say that the sad ghost of the drowned girl still floats in her watery grave.

On one of my visits to Charlecote, as I made my way through the magnificent park as dusk was falling, I thought I caught a glimpse of a girl tripping quickly towards the water but almost as soon as I was aware of the silent, shadowy figure it had disappeared and clearly nothing was where I had just seen 'something'. Was I fortunate enough to catch a fleeting glance of the sad little ghost that still haunts the park at Charlecote? What did I see for which I could find no explanation at the time or during subsequent exploration and inquiry; was it the ethereal, shadowy, silent shade of a desperately sad girl hastening towards the quiet water and there disappearing?

In January 2000 Sir Edmund Fairfax-Lucy announced that he was to fulfil a long cherished dream and create a new Tudor-style topiary garden for the great Elizabethan house. Interference with existing structures has long been known to trigger psychic activity; will the re-introduction of a Tudor garden where one used to exist cause ghosts to return and provide another haunted garden?

CHÂTEAU DE GRATOT
Near Coutances, Normandy, France

Time and again it has been noticed, recorded and verified that restoration, alteration and repair has acted as a trigger to psychic activity. Instances are too numerous to mention but time after time a haunting that has lain dormand for years, centuries even, has taken on a new lease of life following structural alterations. Small wonder then that the Château de Gratot near Coutances, Manche, north-west France, has seen a resurgence of paranormal phenomena after some fifteen years of restoration.

In a volume devoted to ghosts – and how to see them – 'written by the most experienced ghost hunter in the world' (published in 1993), it is stated that the Château de Gratot, a former manor of the Argouges in Normandy, has a haunted tower where the 'ghosts of a man and a woman have been seen on countless occasions and most frequently in bright sunlight.'

The tower in question is known as the Fairy Tower and dates from the fifteenth century. The legendary story, which the official brochure describes as 'neither entirely fiction nor entirely fact . . . but a mixture of literature – the literature of the minstrels – and history – the history of the Argouges,' tells of a lord of the Argouges family of Gratot on his way home from a hunt when his horse, thirsty after the exertions, went towards a pool to drink. As they approached the knight saw a beautiful young woman bathing in the pool. Dismounting, the knight, 'seized with admiration', crept forward as softly as he could but he stepped on a twig and the slight noise startled the girl who fled. During the following days the knight repeatedly visited the pool hoping to catch sight of her again but to no avail.

However at last, one evening, she reappeared as he stood waiting and hoping beside the pool and completely fascinated by her beauty and certain that he was hopelessly in love, he fell on his knees before her, poured out his undying passion and devotion for her and begged her to be his bride. She replied that she was a dryad, of the faery world, but she would agree to become mortal and marry him on one condition: that he never, ever, mentioned the word 'death' in her presence. The lord agreed, the wedding took place, and they enjoyed seven years of happiness.

Then one day the Lord of Gratot was holding a tournament in honour of his cousin, the Lord of Granville. Everyone had arrived and all was ready but the proceedings were delayed by the Lady of Gratot lingering over her toilette. At last, his patience exhausted, the knight went upstairs to find her just coming out of her chamber and he cried: 'Lady, you are so long dressing . . . do you think that Death will tarry too?' Too late he realised the fatal word had been spoken; the faery-wife swayed, let out a piercing cry and vanished through a window. But where she had leaned upon the wall to steady herself she left her handprint in the stone. Everyone remarks upon the worn stairs in the Fairy Tower and legend has it that it is the result of the lord's tears that, day after day and year after year, wore away the stone, rather than the passing of time. At all events the unfortunate faery-lady, being immortal was also doomed to lament her lost happiness and it is said she can still be seen, especially on stormy days, wandering about the Fairy Tower and often glimpsed through the window spaces and sometimes moaning the words that brought about her doom: 'Death! . . . Death!'

Since that tragic day the tower has been called the 'Tour à la Feé' – the Fairy Tower, and the Argouges family adopted 'à la Feé' as their battle cry. The coat of arms of the Argouges immortalised the memory of the fairy-lady and their escutcheon comprises two lions surmounted by a crest with the bust of the fairy-lady with her long tresses springing from the helmet and holding a comb in her right hand and a mirror in her left; a reminder that her toilette was the cause of her downfall.

Once when I visited the Château de Gratot, without knowing anything about any legends or ghosts associated with that lovely spot, I thought, just for a moment, I saw

the forms of a beautiful young lady and an angry man, seemingly dressed in apparel of long, long ago – but it must have been imagination, or so I thought until I heard of other visitors to this remarkable place who had seen and heard things they were totally unable to explain. The haunted gardens at the Château de Gratot draw you back again and again.

Whatever the truth of the legendary tale that is now lost in the mists of time, there does seem to have been the mysterious disappearance of an Argouges lady who had come from a far-off land and who was famous for her beauty. Perhaps legend built on this mysterious disappearance and resulted in a flight of fancy that is regarded by some as the cause or explanation of the Fairy Tower's soaring shape. Whatever the reason, this strange and fascinating tower has been known longer than human memory as the Fairy Tower and there have been witnesses without number who claim to have seen a beautiful young woman with long tresses in the Fairy Tower in bright sunlight – as it probably was when the faery-lady may have disappeared long centuries ago. Can it be, as one castle restoration volunteer said: 'Stone, that incomparable witness, keeps and transmits the message intact'; and as another said, 'Behind architecture and history, or rather inside them, are the men and women who willed and conceived these monuments, those who built them and those who lived in them.' Yet another said, 'an immense strength comes from the Château . . . masses, distances, depths . . . and violence. The power of its granite and moss, of its logic and folly, engulf you.' Whatever the truth of the faery legend and the phantoms that walk there, the Château de Gratot is a truly magical place.

CHENIES MANOR HOUSE
Chenies, near Amersham, Buckinghamshire

Beauty may be in the eye of the beholder but it is also evident in some gardens – even some haunted gardens – and a case in point is the magnificent garden at Chenies Manor near Amersham in Buckinghamshire. Here you can see the State apartment where Queen Elizabeth I slept and where Catherine Howard committed the treason of adultery . . .

It was my friend Alasdair Alpin MacGregor, former Private Secretary to the Chancellor of the Duchy of Lancaster and author of *The Ghost Book* (1955) and *Phantom Footsteps* (1959) among his two dozen books, who first told me about the ghost-infested garden at Chenies Manor House, then recently purchased and occupied by his friends, Alastair MacLeod Matthews and his wife, Elizabeth.

The historic house has fairly complete records going back to the middle of the twelfth-century – although there was then, and perhaps still is, a Royal Oak Tree flourishing that could well be a century and a half older still; certainly it was regarded, when I was first there, as the oldest living thing in Chenies, once called Isenhampstead after the family who owned the manor long, long ago. The records show that at least 130 eggs were once boiled and distributed to the villagers on Easter Day – possibly the first record of Easter eggs in Britain. In 1220, the manor passed to the Cheyne family, whose name is now perpetuated in the area as Chenies. Of that medieval house only the cellars remain, built around 1250 (which we duly explored) and thirty years later the Cheynes forfeited the manor to the Crown.

Thereafter it became the favourite royal retreat of the first three Edwards, three successive Plantagenet kings: Longshanks (who reigned from 1272 to 1307) and who built Caernarvon Castle and instituted the title of Prince of Wales for the heir to the throne; his son (who reigned from 1307 to 1327), who met his match in Robert Bruce at Bannockburn and suffered a painful death in Berkeley Castle; and his son (who reigned from 1327 to 1377) who began the Hundred Years War with France and whose son was Edward, the Black Prince, so-called because of the colour of his armour. All three Edwards knew and loved Chenies Manor House, but towards the end of the fourteenth century the Cheynes were re-established, although they departed once more in 1398 when Sir John Cheyne died in the Tower.

The central portion of the present house is thought, Alasdair told me, to have been built by Edward Molyneux who inherited the property in 1468. In 1528 it passed into the possession of John Russell, first Earl of Bedford (1486-1555) who rebuilt the house ostensibly as we see it today, and it was in Tudor times that Chenies assumed a new importance. The property remained in the Bedford family until the 1950s.

At Chenies are some of England's best examples of Tudor chimneys, twenty-two of them no less, probably the work of the same team of men who worked on Hampton Court for Henry VIII. He was at Chenies several times, with Anne Boleyn in 1534 and with Catherine Howard in 1541 when he may have caught his wife in compromising circumstances with one of his councillors; certainly he tiptoed about the place – as best he could with swollen and painful legs – hoping to surprise the wife he was already tired of and indeed she was beheaded on Tower Green the following year for her indiscretions and adultery. The ghost of King Henry VIII has been reported in the haunted garden at Chenies, the faint and limping footsteps forever seeking his wayward wife.

A volume published in 1995 (*Historic Houses* by Penny Hicks) says of Henry VIII's spectral perambulations: 'They say that his ghostly footsteps can sometimes be heard, painfully dragging his ulcerated legs along in an attempt to catch his queen, Catherine Howard, in the act of adultery with one of his attendants.'

Alastair MacLeod Matthews and his wife Elizabeth moved into Chenies Manor House in 1956 and soon realised that they had ghosts, both inside the house and outside in the garden. They were frequently disturbed in the small hours of the morning by heavy and distinct footfalls and the creaking of floorboards. At first they investigated and traced the sounds to an anteroom of the apartment which Queen Elizabeth I had occupied nearly 400 years before. Could the popular daughter of Henry VIII and Anne Boleyn have entertained admirers at Chenies? In the garden footsteps, sounding as though someone was approaching on a stone path, were frequently heard emanating from the green lawns where there was not a stone in sight. Sometimes the footsteps appeared to be approaching a corner of a well-trimmed hedge but suddenly all sounds cease and nothing can be found to account for the clear sounds heard seconds earlier. Time after time residents and visitors have been deceived by the definite footfalls and invariably they have been surprised and puzzled at the outcome.

Once, Lieutenant-Colonel Matthews told me, he heard limping footsteps outside the bedroom and noticed that the time was just after two o'clock. He got out of bed and quietly followed the sounds. He saw nothing, but the sounds went ahead of him and he followed them to the vicinity of the ancient gallery where two hundred of Cromwell's men once slept. Once too, Lieutenant-Colonel Matthews followed footsteps in the garden but they seemed to fizzle out near an ancient flowerbed.

Once, when the Matthews were making arrangements for some houseguests, it was agreed that they would occupy the Pink Room – until Mrs Matthews pointed out that there was no wardrobe in that room nor a place where one could be conveniently installed.

Her husband then consulted the old plans of the house and noticed that there used to be a small prayer room in the corner of the room above, although there was no corresponding space in the Pink Room. He took precise measurements and they showed that there certainly should be space in the corner of the Pink Room. It was decided to have the wall broken down in the hope that the resulting space would accommodate a wardrobe. The builders broke through two-and-a-half thicknesses of brickwork and found themselves in a space which was in fact a priests' hiding hole. The wall had marked on it a year in the 1660s, the final digit being indistinct but the day was distinct enough: 9th September.

A door was duly hung to the little room and the visitors came and went. Some time later the Matthews children were being fretful and troublesome at night and, as he had a heavy day ahead of him, one night Lieutenant-Colonel Matthews decided to sleep in the Pink Room. It was a very windy night, he recalled, and he read himself to sleep with the help of a candle, for electric light had not then been installed in that part of the house. The newly hung door to the little priests' room was fitted with a 'Suffolk latch', and since the night was boisterous, Matthews made sure that he gave the door a really good pull to and that the latch was down before he settled himself for the night. He was quite certain that the door was absolutely secure and all the windows tightly closed so no breath of wind would extinguish his candle, yet, early in the morning he awoke with the feeling that he was not alone and he found the windows standing wide open and the door to the little secret room also wide open: and when he eventually rose he discovered that the date was 9th September!

During the first few years that they were at Chenies the Matthews discovered other oddities. Alasdair Alpin MacGregor told me that on one of his visits the occupants were busy opening up parts of the house and garden that for years, if not centuries, had been forgotten. Several rooms had been walled-up and in addition to the priests' hiding place they discovered an intriguing sliding panel and, in the garden, something resembling a crypt, which appeared to date from the time when the manor's earliest foundations were laid. Could this have any association, they wondered, with the mysterious footsteps repeatedly reported in the garden, or with the unidentified lady in Elizabethan clothes glimpsed from time to time in the garden.

Just six years after they had taken up residence at Chenies Manor House I took a party of ghost enthusiasts to Chenies and Lieutenant-Colonel MacLeod Matthews, later to become High Sheriff of Buckinghamshire, regaled us with the unique story of the historical and ghostly associations of their beautiful old home and in particular we heard all about the Monks' Walk where a phantom monk had been seen on numerous occasions – although invisible at both ends of the walk – and it is certainly interesting to note that, although none of the Matthews family go out of their way to mention the ghostly attributes of the house and garden, visitors not infrequently ask about the silent monk they have seen, and it invariably turns out to have been on the Monks' Walk.

During our visit one of the party reported seeing a well-attired (although out-of-date) male figure rushing by – seemingly without a head! She was told this would probably be Lord William Russell, an arresting ghost seen periodically. Another saw a ghostly female in the garden, a figure that, although it looked completely real and solid, disappeared abruptly, and when she approached a fellow member of the party whom she had seen almost colliding with the female form, he had seen nothing at all.

Charming Elizabeth and Alastair Matthews, their beautiful home and the exceptionally delightful garden at Chenies Manor House remain lasting memories as does the expectant, waiting atmosphere that pervades that haunted garden.

CLOUDS HILL
Nine miles east of Dorchester, Dorset

Just north of Bovington Army Camp you will find Clouds Hill, a small brick and tile cottage built in 1808 and almost hidden by rhododendrons and shrubbery. It was first rented and then bought by Colonel T. E. Lawrence ('Lawrence of Arabia') when he called himself T. E. Shaw (after his friend George Bernard Shaw) and this is where he retired on leaving the Royal Air Force at the end of February 1935. Less than three months later he was dead but his ghost, in white Arab costume, allegedly haunts the secluded garden.

Lawrence, a private in the Tank Corps in 1923, rented the derelict cottage on the slope of Clouds Hill – the name of the high ground in the vicinity – that year when he was stationed at Bovington Camp. At the time he was without personal ambition, a non-smoker, non-drinker, a vegetarian and without even a bank balance but he needed somewhere to revise and revise and revise again the text of his memorable *Seven Pillars of Wisdom*; a work that was first privately printed in a limited edition in 1926. It was published for general circulation in 1935 and subsequently appeared in numerous editions and styles. My own copy, bound in red leather, embossed and tooled in gold, is one of a limited edition: Lawrence himself would have approved, I feel, as for years he had ideas of finding somewhere in the country to 'build a shed and print books beautifully'.

I am fortunate in having met and known several people who knew 'T. E.' as his friends always called him: Mary Overgaard, with whom he was very close at one time and to whom he gave one of his treasured Arab knives; Herbert White who knew and served with Lawrence on some of his military campaigns; Pat Knowles, his immediate neighbour and friend and with whom he spent his last evening on earth at Clouds Hill; Henry Williamson, whom he visited in Devon and to whom he had just sent a telegram confirming an important meeting when he crashed on his way back to the cottage; and I even met the redoubtable G. B. S. whom he regularly visited at Shaw's Corner in Hertfordshire. Shaw portrayed Lawrence as Private Meek in *Too True To Be Good* and it was Shaw who gave the Brough Superior motorcycle to Lawrence as a gift; 'it was like handing a loaded gun to a would-be suicide' Shaw said afterwards. The Shaws visited Clouds Hill on several occasions but the ghost at Clouds Hill is that of Lawrence while Shaw's ghost walks in the garden at his home at Ayot St Lawrence.

I also talked, on several occasions, with Robert Graves, Lawrence's life-long friend. He told me, 'I knew Lawrence intimately and never had a more generous friend. While it is possible that his inherited Irish imagination may have tempted him at times to coax stories into a more artistic shape than he found them; but at the same time an inherited Scottish conscience always restrained him from wanton lying and I grant you that he would sometimes hide the truth in a misleading statement but people like Sir Ronald Storrs, an old comrade of Lawrence, and such people as Colonel S. F. Newcombe, another of Lawrence's comrades-in-arms, have said, on reading *Seven Pillars*, how it refreshed their memories of various incidents which they personally experienced'. Graves, no stranger to ghosts, told me he thought it 'quite appropriate' that Lawrence should appear after his death in Arab costume at Clouds Hill, thereby fulfilling several accepted requirements for ghostly appearances: his 'apparel was as he most often thought of himself; he appeared at the place he loved more than anywhere in England; and his appearance at all would be in keeping with his outlook on life, death and the power of the human spirit'.

Lawrence made a profound impression on everyone who crossed his path. Leslie Ruth Howard, during the course of her biography of her father, actor Leslie Howard, *A Quite Remarkable Father* (Longmans, Green, 1960) tells of her father accidentally encountering Lawrence polishing the aeroplane that won the Schneider Trophy for Great Britain. Recognising the 'extraordinary Lawrence of Arabia' he thought 'what a strange fellow – after what his life has been, to spend his days polishing an aeroplane . . . odd'.

Mary Overgaard, a long-standing member of The Ghost Club, was instrumental in initiating several investigations including the remarkable Nottingham Council House case in which a paralysed young man, a former resident, apparently responded to the presence, years after his death, of a young lady in the house and subsequently appeared to residents and visitors. The all-night investigation we carried out received considerable publicity and the whole case has been written up by Dennis Bardens (in his *Ghosts and Haunting*, Zeus Press, 1965) and several of my own books including *No Common Task* (Harrap, 1983) and *Nights in Haunted Houses* (Headline, 1994).

Mary Overgaard (as she later became) knew T. E. from the late 1920s until his death. She told me of his 'wonderful', low, quiet voice and his careful and perfect choice of words whenever he spoke. She recalled the times she had sat on the floor with him at Clouds Hill, the gramophone playing in the background and his melodious voice bringing to life his wartime and RAF adventures here and abroad. She said there was something quite magical about T. E. and his meagre cottage and although he never drank anything but water, tea or coffee, he loved fruit, especially apples and after eating all the fruit close to the core, he invariably ate that too, including the pips but he was careful never to eat the stalk. He was known to be a non-smoker (Mary was a heavy cigaratte smoker, incidentally) but she told me that actually he allowed himself two cigarettes a year, one on Christmas Day and one on Easter Day. 'I remember him as incredibly handsome, always shy, unutterably attractive but with a sadness in his soul,' Mary told me. 'After his death I somehow knew he would return in some form and although I was not expecting it, somehow I was not surprised or shocked when I encountered him in his Arab robes when I went to the cottage some time after his death. Pat Knowles was with me and we both saw the unmistakable diminutive figure walk in the way only he could walk towards the door of Clouds Hill and then disappear'.

On no less than three subsequent occasions Mary saw her friend T. E., always in Arab garb, in the haunted garden at Clouds Hill; sometimes when she was alone but once with her sister and Pat Knowles: all three saw the figure at the same time.

Pat Knowles told me he has seen the ghost of Lawrence on five occasions, twice in the company of other people, always in the afternoon and always in the immediate vicinity of his beloved Clouds Hill.

Lawrence's fame produced a wealth of unsolicited letters from unknown people and he always tried to reply, however briefly, (a habit he probably caught from G. B. S. whose brief and witty postcards were renowned), but by the beginning of 1935 he was complaining more and more of the time he spent and the money involved in sending letters to friends and correspondents and he resolved as a New Year resolution to have a card printed stating simply: 'To tell you that in future I shall write few letters'. It was something that obviously worried him, for two years earlier he had told Mary Overgaard, 'upon withdrawal to Clouds Hill I will go through my Address Book and to each name send a printed card saying, "To announce cessation of correspondence".' Like so many of Lawrence's resolutions this one was never acted upon.

Another mutual acquaintance was charming William Buchan, second son of John Buchan (Lord Tweedsmuir) and I treasure the signed copy he gave me of his novel The Blue Pavilions in 1966 when I visited him at his London flat. William Buchan always remembered a visit Lawrence made to Elsfield Manor, near Oxford, the Buchan home, not long before Lawrence's tragic death. William recalled, as he stated in his fascinating book, The Rags of Time – A fragment of Autobiography (1990): 'Lawrence was making one of his surprise visits to Elsfield. My father was away on the day, but my mother and I were at home . . . I can only tell of that morning's encounter as one of memorable charm and easiness which has left a recollection, stronger than most, of something at once pleasurable and deeply sad . . . I see him standing by the tall window in the library, facing me when we talked and giving me every strand of his attention . . .

'He was full of enthusiasm which was almost boyish, an excitement which clearly possessed him completely and gave him a youthful, a holiday air. What he was doing, in fact, was setting out to start on a new way of living.

'We sat in the library, in the mild light of that late spring day, and listened to the plans which Lawrence was about to put into effect. He told us of the bothy in a thicket of rhododendron which from then on was to be his home, his place of retreat, where he hoped to think and read and write in utter peace, free from disturbance by any but his most cherished friends . . . He planned a daily round of the utmost simplicity . . .

'When that unforgettable visit was over, Lawrence mounted his fearsome machine and vanished with a roar up the village street, leaving behind, for memory to lay hold of, the dying growl of a powerful motor and a whiff of caster oil.' And that, I have to say, is very much the way the ghost form of T. E. Lawrence at Clouds Hill has been described to me; bringing with it an air of easiness and charm, at once pleasurable and deeply sad . . .

The great charm he had, still evident it seems in his apparitional form when it is seen at Clouds Hill, was undeniably apparent, especially to the female sex, all his life. Kathleen Scott (widow of Captain Robert Falcon Scott and later Lady Hilton Young) was a considerably talented sculptor. Two kings and four prime ministers were among her subjects but perhaps her best-known work is her statue of her first husband which stands in Waterloo Place in London. Fresh from his triumphs in Arabia, Lawrence went to Kathleen Scott's studio to sit for a marble statuette and she completely fell under his spell. 'Great fun is this lad,' she wrote in her diary. '. . . He has an entrancing humour, subtle as the devil . . .' and later: 'One whole lovely day of Lawrence . . . we worked and talked and had fun.' She seriously considered marriage with Lawrence but after she heard 'hair-raising stories' of his conduct in Arabia, she opted for Edward Hilton Young, the youngest son of Sir George Young. She too would have accepted the possibility of the apparition of Lawrence at Clouds Hill. She left a letter to her son, the naturalist Peter Scott, which she wrote when she thought she was dying, which included the phrase: '. . . remember that if I can see you in any way after I'm dead . . . I shall want to see you gay and merry and funny . . .'

There are still unsolved mysteries surrounding Lawrence's death. The generally accepted story is that at about 11.40 a.m. on 13 May 1935 he was on his way from Bovington Camp to Clouds Hill when, in attempting to avoid colliding with two young cyclists whom he was passing, he swerved, collided with the cyclists and ended up crashing and being thrown up into the air and landing head-first on the road, about 400 yards south of Clouds Hill. He never recovered consciousness and died six days later. Unsolved questions include the speed at which Lawrence was travelling: one witness (who later committed suicide) said his speed was between fifty and sixty miles per hour but subsequent inquiries suggest it was considerably less, perhaps little more than twenty miles per hour; then there was the mysterious black car that one witness insisted he saw but such a car was never traced; there was the conspiracy theory – that Lawrence had been 'removed' because he planned to

visit Hitler; the suggestion that Lawrence was depressed and committed suicide; that the motorcycle developed a fault – all these and other speculations have been put forward but the most likely probability still seems to be that the whole thing was a ghastly accident.

At all events there is considerable evidence that the unmistakable roar of a powerful motorcycle has been heard at various times in the vicinity of the accident; sounds that do not seem to have any rational explanation. And one person told me she is quite convinced that she saw Lawrence, long after his death, on the Brough Superior GW 2275 motorcycle which he so loved to ride in the lanes and roads in this quiet area. Farm workers have heard the noise of the motorcycle roaring towards them in the early hours but always the noise stops abruptly just when the hearer expects to see the perpetrator. Perhaps the last tragic journey that Lawrence took has somehow become imprinted upon the atmosphere. During one of my talks with Lawrence's long-time friend and neighbour, kindly Pat Knowles admitted, somewhat shyly, that he too had heard the roar of Lawrence's machine – which he knew well – and he was always coming across people who claimed to have heard the sound without ever finding a natural explanation.

As I said in my *Gazetter of British Ghosts* (Souvenir Press, 1971) which contained the first published account of any ghostly Lawrence phenomena: 'I have talked with men who served with Lawrence and I like to think that the moving spirit of the Arab revolt does in fact visit again the little cottage he called Clouds Hill where he found some peace at the end of a troubled life.'

T. E. Lawrence or T. E. Shaw, R, and other pseudonyms, call him what you will, the enigmatic Lawrence of Arabia was a complex, sad, divided and depressed but outwardly charming individual – are these the fundamental and required foundations for an apparitional appearance? Yea or nay, as far as human testimony can prove anything, it has proved that the ghostly form of this great man has been seen in the haunted garden at Clouds Hill.

CURRY MALLET MANOR HOUSE
Near Taunton, Somerset

The following is taken from the official report following an investigative visit by members of the Ghost Club Society:

A party of fourteen people spent the night of 23 September 1988 at The Manor House, Curry Mallet, near Taunton in Somerset. Arriving around 4.30 p.m. the party met Mr and Mrs Daniel O'Sullivan, the new owners of the property. At 5.00 p.m. we were invited nearby to meet Mrs Dita Mallet and her daughter and take tea with them. From Mrs Mallet, whose family lived at the manor for some 900 years, we learned something of the history and ghostly associations of the historic manor house where three kings, William the Conqueror, Henry II and King John, had dined in the Great Hall. It is believed that there has been a dwelling place on the site of Curry Mallet Manor House for over 1,000 years; indeed Roman coins and pottery have been found in the immediate vicinity where there is also a Roman well. A Saxon castle, built probably of wood, by Prince Bitric, stood originally on the site.

In 1068 the Mallet family first established their connection with the place when Gilbert, son of William Mallet, Sir de Graville, built a castle on the site of the original Saxon building. The Mallet family is one of the few families that can claim direct descent from a knight or baron who fought at Hastings with the Conqueror – and can prove such a claim, according to Leslie Pine, the acknowledged authority on the period.

Gilbert Mallet was sent to Somerset in 1068 by William the Conqueror to build 'a strong castle' to hold the country against the marauding Welsh and there are many legends associated with the area; among them one concerning the three streams running under the property which it is said are one of the sources of the Holy Well at Glastonbury. One of the daughters of Henry II, Princess Maud, married Gilbert's son. William the Conqueror is reported to have stayed at the castle when he visited Exeter and the West Country; Henry II also stayed here it seems, and King John stayed at the castle on many occasions whilst hunting in the nearby forest and he actually signed state papers during one stay that are now preserved in the State Archives.

Lord William Mallet was one of the barons who rebelled against King John at Runnymead and he stood surety for Magna Carta. In revenge King John had the Pope excommunicate Mallet and all his lands were confiscated, some now being incorporated into the Duchy of Cornwall.

Between the reign of King John (1199-1216) and that of Henry VII (1485-1509) the castle at Curry Mallet seems to have been destroyed and what remained was incorporated into the present manor house. It seems that the castle and about 120 acres were left with the family, for King John himself was godfather to a son of William Mallet and by church law it was not possible to completely dispossess a godson. Curry Mallet was restored by Henry III to William Mallet's daughter, Helewise Mallet, who married Hugh Poyntz. During the Civil War there was considerable damage to the property by Parliamentarian forces who tethered their horses in the Great Hall. During the Monmouth Rebellion Judge Jeffreys, of infamous reputation, hanged one of the Mallets and transported another, to America.

The original water supply, a well, is still situated under the floor of the old Keep, the present panelled Drawing Room, which we used as our Base Room. The present house consists of the Norman Keep, the Great Hall, the Norman Spiral Staircase and later buildings, the present Entrance Hall being erected just before the last war (*c.* 1938) and eliminating an original carriageway that led to the stables, now converted into flats.

Mrs Nita Mallet, then in her late nineties, told us over tea and biscuits in her beautifully furnished sitting room that a number of bodies had been dug up in the manor garden over the years. Our friend Tom Corbett, the clairvoyant, had spent a couple of days at Curry Mallet and had said that while the house had several ghosts, the garden was crowded with them! Nearby Crimson Hill had once been known as Bloody Hill and was said to have run with blood after the slaughterous battle at nearby Sedgemore. There is no doubt that there were many deadly skirmishes in the immediate area resulting in bodies being hastily buried. Among the ghostly episodes long talked about in the locality is the spectral clashing of swords and duellists fighting in Curry Mallet courtyard – especially on one unspecified night of the year.

There have long been stories of a phantom lady at Curry Mallet Manor House, roaming the corridors and garden, and seen by many people, residents and visitors, over the years. She seems to date from Elizabethan times, judging from descriptions of her attire, and she carries keys at her waist and seems house-proud; possibly she is a housekeeper from long ago.

Mrs Mallet also told us about a ghostly Elizabethan man seen in the garden and also inside the old parts of the house; in fact she had herself glimpsed a dapper, slim, sixteenth-century man wearing a ruff; she saw him in the Great Hall, once on the anniversary of the battle of the Armada and she later discovered that at the time of the Armada the then owner of Curry Mallet had repeatedly paced the Great Hall, worried to death over the outcome of that momentous battle. The present owner, Daniel O'Sullivan, told us that these days the Great Hall is sometimes booked for weddings and other family gatherings and recently a band had been engaged to play at a wedding and they had positioned themselves in the Minstrel Gallery overlooking the Great Hall but before long they decamped and came down into the Great Hall and performed there; he never did discover exactly why although there was talk of mysterious figures, snatches of Elizabethan music and inexplicable human forms in old-fashioned apparel. The Great Hall, incidentally, is remarkable and unique for its eleventh-century 'cruck' roof, the oldest existing one of its kind in England.

There have long been stories of a brutal owner of the manor years ago who at one time imprisoned and ill-treated his wife in the end bedroom overlooking the rose garden and here, while attending to some high-growing roses from the bedroom window, Mrs Mallet found herself completely and inexplicably but quite overwhelmingly sad and she felt as though her heart would break; so intense and tremendous was the sudden and puzzling feeling that she has never forgotten it. She said she 'almost' saw a man ill-treating a crying woman in the garden.

Having walked back through the haunted garden to the manor we were taken on a tour of the older parts of Curry Mallet Manor House and in particular the haunted parts. Mr and Mrs O'Sullivan and their family were introduced to all of us and after hearing about our plans for the nocturnal visit they left us to ourselves for the night.

Having discussed all we had learned about the stories associated with the manor we decided to eliminate one corridor near bedrooms occupied by the youngest of the three O'Sullivan children, for fear of disturbing any of the children during the night;

accordingly the two doors leading to this passage were labelled 'Out of Bounds' and were not included in the night's vigil.

While coffee and biscuits were being prepared as a preliminary to getting down to business Member Bob Cato swiftly prepared plans of the two floors detailing the ten rooms we planned to have under surveillance. We decided to position tape recorders in the end bedroom (which we named 'the prison room'); on the Norman Spiral Staircase and in the Great Hall. The fourth machine we decided to keep available for mobile use. Ten thermometers were placed in strategic positions throughout the area and these were checked by a rota of members every twenty minutes: none showed any abnormality throughout the night. We also distributed ten 'control' or 'trigger' objects throughout the rooms and passages and these too were regularly checked by a rota of members every twenty minutes, the times between the thermometer checking and the 'control' objects checking arranged so that there was supervision throughout all the rooms every ten minutes. Among the 'trigger' objects there was some unexplained activity. Beside each thermometer and beside each 'control' object we placed a card appropriately marked to indicate the position of the thermometer or 'control' object and some of these cards were found displaced during the night between patrols. In addition to the thermometer and 'controls' checking there was also a rota of members who carried out 'patrols' every half-hour when members were expected to quietly patrol the whole area and observe and report anything unusual, no matter how trivial. We also instituted three quarter-hour periods of total darkness and total silence, at midnight to 12.15; 2.30 to 2.45 and 4.00 to 4.15 a.m.

Among the puzzling incidents reported during the night were slight movements of a dagger 'trigger' object situated in the courtyard at 10.45 p.m.; the movement in a clockwise direction of approximately five degrees of a photograph 'trigger' object sited in the Minstrel Gallery at 11.42 p.m.; the slight but definite movement from its chalked surround of a crucifix 'trigger' object on the windowsill, overlooking the rose garden in the prison room: at 2.24 a.m.; and the slight movement of a glass paperweight 'trigger' object situated in the shower-room off one bedroom at 10.15 p.m. There was also an unexplained mark made on a piece of paper left in the Entrance Hall. All the objects, after verification, were returned to their chalked outlines. At 10.20 p.m. parts of the garden, near an ancient wall, were found to be unusually cold; this fact was reported by two members and verified by another. A curious clicking sound was heard in the garden by one member and the same sound, loud and distinct, and seemingly quite inexplicable, was reported by another member forty-five minutes later; on both occasions immediate investigation revealed no explanation. At 12.15 two members reported a 'cold area' in the middle of the lawn and this was verified by another member and by thermometer.

During the midnight to 12.15 'silence' period a creaking or squeaking sound was heard intermittently in the back garden for the whole quarter-hour period and in fact over almost half-an-hour; it seemed to originate behind a yew tree and the sound seemed to be localised although no material cause could be found. It was heard by two members, verified by two others, and subsequently established that it was not due to birds or the trees themselves. It was recorded on tape. During the 2.30 to 2.45 'silence' period there was complete silence throughout the whole area under surveillance, including the garden, although our instruments established that in fact the wind was higher than two hours previously. At the end of the 'silence' period the sound of the wind resumed: both the sound and the silence was recorded.

During the 2.30 to 2.45 'silence' period a single word that sounded like a drawn-out 'Ju-lee' was heard in the courtyard by two members, seeming to originate from the back garden. Two members there heard nothing. The same word at the same time was heard by one member apparently emanating from the Base Room, which overlooked the back garden; nothing was heard by two members in the Base Room at the time. A faint sound of whispering was heard twice in the vicinity of the Entrance Hall by one member. Also during this period a curious 'creaking' sound was reported: it was loud enough to cause two members to turn round simultaneously while on duty in the courtyard – an area several members felt to be one of the most 'interesting' parts of the whole house. At 2.40 a.m. a 'very strong odour' of fresh earth was reported by one member at the top of the Norman Spiral Staircase, four or five feet in area and it lasted about one minute. A very similar smell was reported from the same place at 3.00 a.m. by a different member. Between 3.00 and 3.05 a.m. the card indicating Thermometer No. 5 (situated beside the appropriate thermometer on the windowsill of the 'prison room') was discovered to have moved three feet(!). It had remained unmoved and in position from 11.00 p.m. until 3.00 a.m. It was discovered by one member and verified by two others. At 4.30 a.m. a button was discovered on a table in the Base Room. It was unclaimed and did not appear to have belonged to any member present although it was certainly not there a few minutes earlier. It was of comparatively recent design. (Later, we asked the O'Sullivans but they had no knowledge of the button).

At 4.15 a.m. and later a light in the Minstrel Gallery went on and off intermittently for the rest of our sojourn, until Council Member Trevor Kenward discovered that it was part of the security set-up and was triggered by sound – this was later confirmed by Mr O'Sullivan who said he had overlooked turning if off the night before. Interestingly enough on the first occasion the light seemed to be triggered by a pencil falling from the deep window recess in the Minstrel Gallery, although it seemed to be established afterwards that the sound caused by a pencil falling was insufficient to trigger the light. A piece of paper, as well as the pencil, was discovered moved in this immediate area but it was felt that a draught from the window could have caused these movements. Mr O'Sullivan did not tell us about the band moving from the Minstrel Gallery until the morning after our night's vigil although several members had remarked on the curious atmosphere in the gallery that was not noticed elsewhere. It was reported that several members felt very cold in this part of the manor house and during the night two raps, a rattling noise, an occasional 'click' and a heavy, regulated rustling sound – almost like footfalls – were recorded when the area was deserted; the recordings being played back at 4.40 a.m.

During the course of an impromptu séance at 3.00 a.m. various sounds were heard and 'messages' received. Opening the attempted communication the organiser asked, 'Can I help you?' and immediately there was a loud rushing of wind down the nearby chimney and exactly the same thing happened at 3.16 a.m. when the question was asked, 'Can we help you?' One minute earlier a single ringing sound was heard. 'Messages' seemed to suggest that the communicating entity was a former inhabitant who lived in the 1600s, possibly the figure seen by Mrs Mallet and others and 'he' said he preferred the garden. This entity gave his initials as R.F. and said he died in the garden and his remains had been disturbed. He went on to say he was murdered and that he was a Mallet. The entity repeated that he was murdered in the garden and buried there; adding that there were other 'spirits' in the garden and also in the house, but most were in the garden. Asked to manifest in some way, such as moving a ringed object, the entity agreed to try and this was prior to the movement of the thermometer card in the 'prison room'. Further 'messages' suggested that the murdered person was a lover of the mistress of the house and when the couple were discovered together they were both murdered by a Mallet, in the garden. The initials R.F. were verified several times and it was stated that there was something in the house bearing these initials.

During a second séance at 4.00 a.m. R.F. seemed reluctant to communicate and things were abandoned for a few minutes. At 4.10 a.m. the third attempted séance began with an entity who accepted R.F. as his initials but nothing of great moment transpired. A fourth attempt at 4.30 a.m. had R.F. claiming to have left a message and to have been responsible for moving the thermometer card, and to have produced the button. The entity said he would speak into a tape recorder but he does not appear to have done so. Eventually the entity promoted violent movement of a wine glass and he seemed to agree with everything put to him. The séance was halted. The fifth and final séance began at 4.50 a.m. and again there was a great rushing of wind when the opening question, 'Can we help you?' was asked; but the control seemed tired and when asked, 'Shall we stop?' the answer came 'Yes' so that attempted séance was closed – and again there was a rushing wind down the chimney! All the séances were held in the Base Room (the panelled Drawing Room) in front of an enormous fireplace.

After the investigative visit came to an end it was discovered by one member that a recording machine positioned in the room leading from the panelled Drawing Room to the stone Norman Spiral Staircase had had its cassette turned. Side 1 which had been inserted to play was found to have nothing on it but Side 2 had been inserted to play; to do this it would have been necessary to rewind the cassette.

The night at Curry Mallet Manor House was very interesting both from a historical and from a psychic point of view. Objects were moved; odd sounds were heard; an apparently disembodied voice was heard at the same time from three positions and not from other, apparently nearer, positions. There was a definite 'atmosphere' in parts of the house throughout most of the night and this was reflected in the fact that no member of the party felt in the least tired throughout the whole night (apart from one member who developed a heavy cold) and there was an overall air of expectancy, a feeling that something might happen at any moment and we were all greatly indebted to Mr and Mrs O'Sullivan for their kindnesses and their thoughtfulness and their co-operation in allowing us to spend a night in such a beautiful, historic, alive and utterly charming manor house and its equally charming and equally haunted garden.

Members taking part in this at times exciting exercise in practical psychical investigation were, in alphabetical order, Bob Cato (Edinburgh), Mavis Don (Seaford), Ruth Jarvis (Rainham), Marilyn and Trevor Kenward (Verwood), Tim Miller (Leigh-on-Sea), Philip Moore (Seaford), Dennis Moyses (Peterborough), Lynda Randall (Tonbridge), Shirley Shaw (Lindfield), Michael Sweetman (Plymouth), Joyce and Peter Underwood (Bentley) and Michael Williams (St Teath, Cornwall).

EARLSHALL CASTLE
Leuchars, near St Andrews, Fife, Scotland

I heard all about the hauntings at Earlshall Castle when it was owned and occupied by Major D. R. Baxter, the Laird of Earlshall, who, sadly due to health reasons, had to sell Earlshall in 1996. The Baron of Earlshall, whose ancestor was Sir William Bruce who built the castle in 1546, was always careful to ensure that the historic and impressive castle was unchanged and unspoiled by any subsequent 'improvements' and the half-panelled room where Mary Queen of Scots (1542-1587) stayed was faithfully preserved – perhaps because it was said to harbour the ghost of a little old lady, possibly a servant from days gone by; and where the unused bed was frequently found to be depressed as though someone had slept there: could this be the invisible but tangible ghost of the Queen of Scotland and Queen-Consort of France; she was married at an early age to the dauphin of France, son of Henry II. Her husband became King of France in 1559 but died in the following year. A woman of intense personal charm, intelligent and courageous it seems appropriate that she should haunt such a gem of a castle as Earlshall.

Her ghost has been seen in the haunted garden here and animals – 'good psychic barometers' Elliott O'Donnell used to say – have long been aware of 'something' at a certain spot; the Earl told me the family dogs would never willingly go near but stand and stare at something that nobody else could see. The Official Guide (dated 1985) has other ideas: 'It would be nice to think that Robert Mackenzie and his wife Jessie stroll in the gardens that they reclaimed from a wilderness and which they loved

so much'. Personally I have talked with visitors to Earlshall who are convinced that they have seen the ghostly form of a regal young woman composed, compassionate and beautiful, with an air about her of a fearless and frank simplicity and a genuine pleasure in the peace of a garden; this certainly sounds like the passionate queen who three months and six days after the murder of her husband became the wife of her husband's murderer. Undoubtedly Mary Queen of Scots had all the attributes allegedly necessary for ghostly appearances and it must seem likely that she walks occasionally in the pleasant gardens of Earlshall as she assuredly walks at Stirling Castle, the Talbot Hotel at Oundle, Sawston Hall, the Turret House at Sheffield, Temple Newsam, Leeds, Nappa Hall, Wensleydale, and massive Hermitage Castle. Certainly she must have looked out across these beautiful gardens after a day's hunting as she changed from her riding habit in the small, half-panelled bedchamber here still known as Mary Queen of Scots' Room. She was nineteen when she visited Earlshall in 1561.

In 1998 the Baron of Earlshall informed me in writing that the ghostly footsteps of his ancestor Sir Andrew Bruce – Bloody Bruce, 'a wicked and violent persecutor' according to a contemporary report, were frequently heard ascending and descending the main spiral staircase. 'All members of the family heard him from time to time, as well as significant numbers of the staff, guides and visitors'. His letter continues: 'Regarding the gardens, our dog when young used to sit at a certain spot and his head would move as if he were following the movement of someone or something: he resolutely refused to walk along that particular path. Ben is still with us, now fourteen-and-a-half years old, arthritic, stone deaf and with poor eyesight, but as game – and as cantankerous – as he has always been.

'Flo, one of our guides, swears that one day she saw a woman in long black clothes apparently walk through the holly hedge bordering the Yew Lawn. Another, apparent, garden manifestation occurred when we were open to the public and three middle-aged ladies, who had been walking in the gardens, rushed back into the castle and asked to speak to one of our guides, Mrs Betty Caseby. One of the women was clearly very agitated and asked Betty if the castle was haunted (I presume that they didn't have a guide book, or, at least, had not looked at it). Betty recounted the tales of the Bloody Bruce but she was interrupted by the woman saying, "No, what I mean is, are there any ghosts in the gardens?" and she went on to say that the three of them had been walking along the path bordering the Yew Lawn, chatting away, when she had looked up and seen – as she described it – a disembodied head of an old woman in front of her. She said she was speechless but tried to draw the attention of her companions to what she was witnessing. However, even as she tried to draw her friends' attention to the phenomenon, it slowly faded away. In her own words, "I never did believe in ghosts – but I do now!"'

The origin of the name Earlshall is lost in the mists of antiquity but tradition has it that it takes its name from the site of a hunting lodge, 'the Earl's Hall' owned by the ancient Earls of Fife. The land is first recorded as being owned by the powerful Anglo-Norman family of de Quincey, Earls of Winchester during the reign of William the Lion, King of Scotland from 1165 to 1214. The gardens, both those that are haunted and those that are deserted, were rescued from oblivion by the Baroness of Earlshall in the late 1980s and early 1990s enjoying something of a renaissance from a parlous state to being opened for Scotland's Garden Scheme and it may be that this restoring and bringing back the beauty of the gardens has been instrumental in giving new life to the phantoms and spectres of a past age. It is acknowledged that alterations to buildings often affects ghostly manifestations and it does not seem beyond possibility that the haunted gardens at Earlshall owe something to the love and renovation meted out to them for a decade or more.

As Sir Robert Lorimer said about Earlshall: 'The natural park comes up to the walls of the house on one side, on the other you stroll out into the enclosed garden.

That is all – a house and a garden enclosed, but what a promise can such a place be made! Such surprises – little gardens within the garden: the Months Garden, the Herb Garden, the Yew Valley . . . great interesting walls of shaven grass on either side borders of the brightest flowers backed by low espaliers hanging with shining apples and within these espaliers again the gardener has his kingdom!' Small wonder that even the ghosts cannot resist returning to the haunted gardens of Earlshall.

Perhaps a last word from Major Baxter, Baron of Earlshall: 'I am sure that people who have a great love or affinity for a place which has played a special part in their lifetime will, even after their death, continue to imprint their personality, possibly in a personalised form. If my theory holds good, then a hundred or more years from now, people will see my wife and myself in the gardens at Earlshall. Certainly, as I was fond of telling our guides, the spirits of our ancestors are not so far away and a hundred years from now, when smoking will have been outlawed, residents and visitors at Earlshall will smell the strong cigar smoke of a long dead laird (myself!).'

EDZELL CASTLE
Edzell, near Brechin, Angus, Scotland

'The fine old castle of Edzell' as S. P. B. Mais called it, has unique historic associations and wonderful haunted gardens. The oldest part of the castle, the square Stirling Tower, with the bower used by Mary Queen of Scots during her visits to Edzell has been preserved more or less intact while the lower Round Tower is much damaged and the connecting range built by the Lindsays and formerly the state apartments, is now a mere shell. The keep overlooks a square enclosure, once the flower garden or 'viridarium' of Sir David Lindsay, whose arms and the date 1604 appear over a doorway in the north-east corner. The walls are decorated, with bas-reliefs of the virtues, sciences and planets and are indented with large square holes which, from a distance, are seen to form, in combination with the mullets surmounting them, the Lindsay coat of arms. In the angle of this court is a turreted garden house of the same date. I must acknowledge considerable help from researcher and author Norman Adams for information about Edzell Castle and its garden with a ghost.

Edzell Castle is located less than a mile west of Edzell village and six miles north of the cathedral city of Brechin in Angus. An earlier castle, which stood near the present castle, was sold by Stirling of Glenesk to the Crawford Lindsays in 1357.

The red and ruined castle of Edzell was the home of the Lindsay family from the fifteenth century to the middle of the eighteenth century. The tower house overlooks a magnificent pleasance, or walled garden, which was created in 1604. Mary Queen of Scots lodged at the castle in August 1562, when a Privy Council was held there.

The Queen's army was heading northwards to crush a rebellion led by the 4th Earl of Huntly, at the Battle of Corrichie (28 October 1562), near Banchory. Her son, James VI of Scotland, visited Edzell twice during his reign. On his second visit, in August 1589, he received the submission of the Catholic Earl of Erroll, and heard that Henry III of France had been assassinated.

The Lindsays were known as the 'lichtsome Lindsays' because of their gifted, gallant and carefree nature. But they were not businessmen. Their estates were badly managed and when Sir David Lindsay, Lord Edzell, died in 1610, he left the family in debt. The estates were sold to Lord Panmure in 1715, the year of the first Jacobite rebellion. The new owner, a staunch Jacobite, joined the uprising and his land was forfeited as a result. After the Forty-Five Uprising the estate and castle fell into ruin and decay but were later bought back by William Maule, Earl of Panmure of Forth. In the 1930s the castle and environs were handed over by Lord Dalhousie to the care of Historic Scotland.

The pleasance really does have many outstanding features, Norman Adams tells me, including sculptured panels depicting the planetary deities, liberal arts and cardinal virtues already referred to. Trim boxwood hedges and heraldic stones spell out the Lindsay family motto: *Dum Spiro Spero* (While I Breathe I Hope).

The castle and garden are haunted by the White Lady of Edzell, believed to be the ghost of Catherine Campbell, the second wife of David Lindsay, 9th Earl of Crawford. When her husband died she was said to be the richest widow in Scotland. The Lady of Edzell was visiting Brechin Castle in October 1578 when she became ill and was pronounced dead by physicians. But tradition has it that she was epileptic and had fallen into a deep coma. Her body was wrapped in a shroud and draped in her favourite jewellery before being conveyed to the family chapel in Edzell Cemetery, a short distance to the south-west of the castle. The deathwatch was overseen by a sexton on the nights before Lady Edzell was placed in the vault below. On the eve of the burial this man, his grief overcome by greed, attempted to steal some of the precious gems. As he interfered with her the good lady gave a deep groan and awoke from her coma. She promised the sexton he could keep the jewels if he would conduct her back to the castle – but the thief fled into the cold night. Somehow Catherine dragged her weakened frame back to the castle and pleaded with the guards to open the gates. But they feared witchcraft and refused. By first light Lady Edzell was dead from exposure. The sexton was eventually hanged.

In February 1987 a gardener, David Jamieson, came face to face with the White Lady when he unlocked the door connecting the turreted summerhouse with the garden. 'I was frozen with fear,' Mr Jamieson told Norman Adams. 'A few paces in front of me stood something resembling a piece of white lace. When I stepped forward it moved backwards. When I stopped it stopped. It was a little taller than me and gave off a horrible sickly smell like strong pipe tobacco. After a few seconds it vanished. Exactly what it was I don't know. I was very frightened – but it was not evil.'

At certain times of the year fog clings to the Angus landscape but Mr Jamieson denied the 'thing' was nothing but a wisp of fog. When he mentioned his strange experience to a visiting psychic she suggested that the smell he detected might have been due to embalming fluid.

Mr Geoff Hutson, a former castle curator, claimed he saw the White Lady on two occasions in 1986. Their paths crossed the first time in the garden. No one had visited the castle on that particular day and he was surprised when he caught a glimpse of the figure walking along a footpath. A few weeks later the apparition appeared in a field north of the castle. He spotted her again in the courtyard in September 1993. The figure wore old-fashioned clothes – a white flowing dress with billowing sleeves. Her face was distorted; a blur. 'There was an odour,' he said, 'a smell of scent, but she didn't make a sound as she moved. The first time I saw her it felt a little strange.' The apparition of the White Lady of Edzell has also been seen near the family vault.

El Greco's House-Museum
Toledo, Spain

It has been said that the paintings of El Greco (real name Domenico Theotocopuli) show him to have been an intimate, austere, lonely, ardent and mystic personality. 'Neither the life nor the works were those of a normal man,' says art expert, Antonico J. Onieva. Born on the Isle of Crete in 1541, he died in 1614 in Toledo, then the shrine of the mystery and chivalry of old Spain, where he had resided for over thirty years, where, as well as painting some of the most admired works of art in the world he designed the architecture and sculpture of at least one composite altar in the Venetian style and painted the pictures for it: the Church of St Dominic the Antiguo, on the outskirts of the city. He never lacked work, earned plenty of money and painted until his last days. He was buried in a vault in his beloved Church of St Dominic the Antiguo from which his remains passed to the Church of San Torcuato which was destroyed and El Greco's remains were lost.

The ghost in El Greco's lovely garden – built on the foundations of a former mansion – is that of a sad-looking senhorita. There is evidence to suggest that El Greco was terrified by open spaces and that he encountered the ghost in his garden and possibly other spectres for some of the characters in his paintings closely resemble ghosts; perhaps especially the shepherds in 'The Adoration of the Shepherds' where the Virgin is lifting the veil that covers her son to allow the shepherds to contemplate Him, and is bathed in brightness. This same brightness makes the shepherds look like ghosts. Some of his contemporaries thought El Greco mad; and he certainly suffered

religious strife, tumult, agony and mystic absorption – according to the *Encyclopedia Britannica*.

El Greco's masterpiece, one of the world's greatest pictures, 'The Burial of Count Orgaz' was painted in 1587 for Toledo's Church of Santo Tome with its beautiful Mudejar tower and the picture is a posthumous homage to the Count of Orgaz, Don Gonzala Ruiz de Toledo, a pious man who dedicated a great deal of wealth to the services of the churches. It has been said that El Greco's paintings, always stormy and mystical, with their foreshortened or strangely elongated figures, vehemently express the painter's spiritual intentions. By reducing his palette to just five colours, he used these few pigments to intense and dramatic effect.

The so-called House-Museum of El Greco, together with the courtyard and haunted garden, is the most complete example of a Toledo house, 'preserved in all its ornamental and architectonic elements with the utmost integrity'; the reconstruction of the seventeenth-century atmosphere and decoration make this one of the most propitiate and most treasured places for tourists; it may also have played a part in the manifestation that has long been reported here. The majority of El Greco's portrait paintings are of men but beautiful women sought him out to paint them for posterity and one wonders whether the beautiful but sad-looking senhorita who has been seen on so many occasions in the El Greco garden is such a person.

When I was there in 1990 the curator told me he had seen the phantom four times and he had records of the mysterious form being seen on more than a score of occasions, frequently accompanied by a feeling of great sadness. Only last year when a friend told me he was visiting Toledo and was looking forward to seeing the splendid house and museum of El Greco, I suggested he explore the garden and spend a quiet moment there contemplating the occupant of four centuries earlier. When he returned he told me how much he had enjoyed the visit, especially the atmospheric interior of El Greco's house and the garden where, as he quietly contemplated the past, as I had suggested, he became aware of a lady standing looking at him from the other end of the garden. She was dressed in oddly traditional but out-of-date costume and as he approached she suddenly disappeared. No one inside the house could tell him who she might have been but he noticed quiet looks pass between staff members as though this was not the first time they had been faced with this mystery visitor.

The quiet ghost in El Greco's garden is another harmless shade from the past and is probably only viewed from one particular spot on any particular occasion.

FORT MONROE
Virginia, USA

This old, heptagon-shaped, stone fortress is surrounded by a deep moat and a number of Civil War ghosts reputedly haunt these grounds. In particular the gardens seemingly harbour ghosts, so much so that one area, the vicinity of Matthew Lane, has become known as Ghost Alley. There is a very curious atmosphere there and in other parts of the grounds that has been remarked upon by visitors unfamiliar with the history or the reputation of the place.

Fort Monroe was designed by Brigadier General Simon Bernard, the noted French military engineer and former aide to the Emperor Napoleon I. Construction began in 1819 and was completed in 1834. Comprising sixty-three acres Fort Monroe is

the largest enclosed fortification in the country. Standing on the tip of Old Point Comfort, a flat sand spit some two-and-a-half miles long projecting southwards from the mainland and separated by Mill Creek, Old Point Comfort was easily defended and difficult to approach. Close to the Point on the seaward side the main channel runs from Chesapeake Bay into Hampston Roads and the channel is dominated and controlled by Fort Monroe, hence the designation 'the Gibraltar of Chesapeake Bay'. The crowning glory of Fort Monroe's grounds is the beautiful line of oak trees which are lovingly tended and cared for by the military authorities; they are thought to be some of the oldest living oaks in the United States. Tree experts believe these trees were probably there when the first colonists arrived; if so they saw Captain John Smith explore Old Point Comfort in 1608. There is a theory that wood, and especially ancient wood, sometimes has the ability to preserve, almost like a camera, events and under certain conditions to contribute to the reappearance of long-past happenings. It could well be that these beautiful trees play a part in the enduring psychic manifestations that have been reported from Fort Monroe; a fortress that has been manned longer than any other post in the United States. Here was the first permanent English settlement in North America and Sir Walter Raleigh named it 'Virginia' in honour of Queen Elizabeth who was known as 'the virgin queen'.

Some of the gardens, the grassy areas and certainly the vicinity of some of the trees exude a disturbing influence and visitors and residents find themselves recalling some of the history and the historic figures associated with Fort Monroe with alarming clarity.

VIRGINIA PENINSULA

FORT MONROE

General Robert E. Lee, whose haunted boyhood home at Alexandria in the north-west corner of the state, is one ghost reportedly seen here; others include the ghosts of Abraham Lincoln, General Lafayette and Ulysses S. Grant: all haunt the Old Quarters, inside and outside; while according to Richard Winer, also occasionally walking here are the ghosts of Chief Black Hawk, Edgar Allan Poe, Captain John Smith of Pocahontas fame, George Washington and Jefferson Davis who, after the Civil War, was shackled and imprisoned in a cell in the Casemate. The ghostly form of his wife, Varina Lee, has also been glimpsed from time to time looking out of a bedroom window, plump and unmistakable, across from the cell where her husband was imprisoned.

Then there is the ghost of Camille Kirtz, sometimes known as 'The White Lady' for this phantom appears to be luminous, emitting a white light, and she has been seen most often in the place where her husband caught her in the embrace of a Frenchman. Captain Wilhelm Kirtz pulled out his gun to shoot the Frenchman but instead the bullet entered his wife's body below the left breast, and penetrated her heart. The couple had lived and loved at the nearby Tuileries, the officers' quarters, and the strangely luminous figure of Camille still haunts the place where she knew happiness and horror at the same time. Extreme happiness sometimes has the effect of leaving behind a visible presence of the person concerned; horror, surprise and sudden death also sometimes trigger apparitional forms: when all these components are fused together, little wonder that we have a striking luminous spectre.

Muriel Hankey, a very experienced psychical researcher, author and herself psychic, told me that she saw in good afternoon daylight a distinct figure seemingly emerge from the shadows of some trees at Fort Monroe. The clothes of the seemingly solid and genuine masculine figure were very out of date but she immediately thought she recognised the gentlemanly form with sparse hair and tapering moustache – surely it was none other than Edgar Allan Poe, the man who was fascinated yet terrified by death – no tale of his is without the element of death and he was no stranger to it. He witnessed the 1832 cholera epidemic in New York and for five years he was obliged to watch his child-wife die of consumption. He was at Fort Monroe for just four months, from 15 December 1828 to 15 April 1829. Muriel told me she wondered whether Poe manifested to her because she was English; he always had a soft spot for English people having been partly educated at an English public school which he never forgot. Later he attended the University of Virginia and then enlisted in the Army. Fort Monroe seems to have an attraction for him that even death cannot quell.

Edgar Allan Poe was always proud of his faultless logic and it cannot but be interesting that his ghost, if that is what it is, always appears and disappears in a logical way for a ghost. Within seconds, the figure, as Muriel approached, seemed to melt back into the trees and quickly vanished completely. Muriel subsequently spoke to four people at Fort Monroe who had seen the same figure in the same place.

Other reliable people who have told me they have seen ghosts at Fort Monroe include clairvoyant Jeanne Dixon; Professor Alun R. Jones; Dr Grace Thornton and Robert Aickman, creator of the Inlands Waterways Association. Like Muriel Hankey they had visited historic Fort Monroe – many of the buildings are open to the public – without knowing anything about any ghosts there.

GAULDEN MANOR
Tolland, Somerset

There is something about Somerset with its million acres of rolling countryside, its remarkable and historic houses, many with ghostly associations, and none more romantic, charming and haunted than Gaulden Manor.

Here, in a house immortalised by Thomas Hardy and the ghostly Turberville coach, Mr and Mrs James Le Gendre Starkie on my first visit there showed me over their wonderful home and its haunted garden. They have created a really delightful home and truly charming gardens in the thirty years they have been at Gaulden.

Gaulden Manor has a history going back more than 800 years; originally called Gaveldon and then Gaulden, Galden, Golden and finally back to Gaulden, which is a contraction of the original Gaveldon and is pronounced 'Golden'. In about 1199, during the reign of King John, one Andrew de Bovedon is recorded as giving

Gaulden-in-Tolland to the priory of nearby Taunton. The property was already described as a manor with the customary rents, services and domestic lands and perquisites of courts and, while in the possession of Taunton Priory, there seems to have been a grange or house at Gaulden which was sometimes visited by the chief prior who took charge of such rents. Research at Somerset Records Office shows a manor court being held at Gaulden in 1319. In the grounds there was a large pond which provided the monks with fish and the same pond can be seen today, together with a bank of old-fashioned rose trees, a Scent Garden, a Butterfly Garden, a Bog Garden and an enclosed Secret Garden.

After the dissolution of the monasteries by King Henry VIII the Act of Suppression in 1539 brought the larger monasteries into the King's hands and the properties were acquired by nobles, Gaulden eventually being granted to William Standysh for life in 1545. On his death in 1551 the manor passed to Francis Southwell who, in 1565, sold it to George Mynne and it was around this time that a number of historical writers believe that Gaulden Manor became the retreat of the ex-Bishop of Exeter, James Turberville. He had been imprisoned in the Tower with five other bishops for not taking the Oath of Supremacy to Queen Elizabeth in 1559. Two years after his release (in 1563) into the care of the Protestant Bishop of London, he appears to have left London and lived quietly for the rest of his life at Gaulden Manor. Today, over the great fireplace in the Great Hall can be seen the Turberville arms. As late as 1746 there is reference in a will to 'my daughter Turberville of Tolland' and a George Turberville who owned the manor, together with those of Hocombe and Pyleigh in 1751.

Thomas Hardy has immortalised the Turberville family and the Le Gendre Starkies told me in 1984 that the house had long had the reputation of having been visited on many occasions by the phantom Turberville Coach, but such visits supposedly presaged the death of a member of that illustrious family and since there were no longer any Turbervilles at Gaulden Manor, it may no longer have a phantom coach; be that as it may, there are certainly other ghosts at Gaulden. Indeed, where shall we start? With the phantom monks, the ghostly Grey Lady, the unidentified ghost of a small lady or the three ghostly cavaliers – not to mention the knockings and rappings and unexplained footsteps and other phantom forms only ever seen fleetingly.

That there are monks buried in the garden at Gaulden seems very likely (local people have always said so, for generations) and folk memory talks of a secret passage in the garden that leads towards Wivelscombe and another towards the old buildings at Grove Farm which is reputed to have once been a nunnery. Ghosts of phantom clerics have been seen 'on many occasions in the past' (according to one author) so often in one part of the garden that it has been suggested that may be the reason it has become known as the Bishop's Garden. Once, when I was at Gaulden making a television film about the ghosts there, James Le Gendre Starkie donned a monk's cloak and cowl and walked through the Bishop's Garden for the cameras. One member of the camera crew swore he had seen a second 'monk' following the owner-actor and thought another actor had been employed – but the second figure suddenly and inexplicably vanished and it then transpired that no one else had seen the 'phantom' monk, if that was what it was.

Near the main entrance of Gaulden Manor, sometimes inside near the front stairs and sometimes outside in the garden various people have reported seeing the figure of a small woman who is there one minute and not there the next. No one knows who she is or was or why she haunts the place, but evidence extends well beyond living memory right up to the present day. Once when my wife and I were at Gaulden, she left about eleven o'clock one morning to explore the antique shops of the area and returned around 3.30 p.m. Almost as soon as she was inside the house Mrs Hunter, who is no stranger to Gaulden and sometimes helps in the house, asked my wife whether she had changed clothes and returned to Gaulden Manor at lunch time, which of course she had not done, but Mrs Hunter then revealed that she had been working in the dining-room and had looked up around noon and had seen a lady with dark hair and wearing a blue costume of some sort standing in the hall by the front door. After a moment the figure was no longer there. My wife's dark hair and her general size suggested to Mrs Hunter that she was the only person it could have been, the only person at Gaulden Manor that day who looked anything like the figure she had seen; but my wife was not wearing a blue outfit on that occasion and in any case she was miles away from Gaulden Manor at noon.

Incidentally Mrs Hunter, and her daughter too, have seen ghosts at Gaulden, and a former housekeeper often told of seeing the form of a ghost monk inside the manor and in the garden.

The ghostly Grey Lady of Gaulden has also been glimpsed in the garden, a harmless phantom walking where perhaps she used to walk – and invariably disappearing whenever anyone gets too close. She had been seen inside the manor sitting on the right-hand side of the fireplace in the Great Hall and a former owner found that she also haunted one bedroom so consistently that he locked and shuttered the room and kept it that way because he was asked so many questions about the identity of the Grey Lady who, in common with many housebound phantoms, seems to be visible one minute and gone the next.

It would seem that there is a ghost dog in the garden too. In a letter to me Mrs Le Gendre Starkie says: 'We look forward to your visit – I must tell you a new – perhaps ghost – story. A few months ago a black and white chihuahua was buried in the garden (a dog sold by me to a friend, author Rosemary Weir, and buried by request near his father, whose statue is in the garden). A visitor, a girl of about ten years, came into the shop last week and said, "I have just seen a little black and white dog go into the hedge". At the time I had a tan-coloured chihuahua on my lap. The girl said: "A dog like that". I said, "Perhaps it was a rabbit?" "No," she replied. "It was a little dog like yours but black and white." The owner of the dog was nearly demented when he died and other dogs are not allowed here when we are open to the public and all my dogs were shut up. Was it a ghost?'

The Great Hall, with its magnificent plasterwork installed by James Turberville and with the Turberville coat of arms over the Tudor fireplace, is haunted by the frightening manifestation of three cavaliers standing in front of the carved seventeenth-century oak screen, seemingly covered in blood!

103

On the first occasion that Mrs Le Gendre Starkie showed us the Great Hall, my wife and I were quietly admiring the extensive plasterwork with various biblical scenes, including the roundels of King David with his harp and the Angel of Death blowing a trumpet over a skeleton, when Mrs Starkie asked my wife whether she liked the room and my wife, at that time examining the carved oak screen, replied that she felt something very unpleasant had happened in the immediate area of the carved panels.

Mrs Starkie then told us that there had been a battle near Gaulden during the Civil War and it was more than likely that some wounded cavaliers were received at Gaulden, quite possibly badly wounded and bleeding, perhaps even dying, and it could well be that perhaps leaving this life in such a traumatic state, they had left behind 'something' that some people can detect hundreds of years later. Mrs Starkie added that it was known that Cromwell's men were at Gaulden for over a week on one occasion, perhaps seeking fugitive cavaliers who were hiding at Gaulden Manor. One visitor to the manor, evidently sensitive to such things, said as he was about to walk into the Great Hall that he could see three cavaliers standing in front of the carved panels, covered in blood, and he refused to enter the room. Another visitor, a responsible schoolmaster, has found that there is always 'something frightening' about the Great Hall.

As for the delightful owners, Mr and Mrs James Le Gendre Starkie – well, they have heard footsteps mounting the main staircase at night, very loud and distinct footsteps, but there is never any sound continuing beyond the top of the stairs and nothing has ever been found that might account for the sounds.

Hugh Massingbred visited Gaulden Manor in 1995 and said afterwards: 'Ghosts or no ghosts I found myself enchanted by Gaulden's cosy embrace. As Jean Le Starkie says: "We find the house has a pleasant and warm atmosphere – and if there are any ghosts here, they are friendly ones".'

At the top of the stairs the Turberville Bedroom with its enormous Turberville coat of arms in plaster over the fine Tudor fireplace and its majestic four-poster, is reputedly haunted and in this, to my mind, very pleasant room, ghosts have been seen recently.

But it is the garden, or rather the gardens, at Gaulden Manor that are especially haunted and, for those with eyes to see and ears to hear, the shades of past occupants still wander these ancient paths and lawns, taking one back in the mind's eye to days long past but not forgotten at gorgeous Gaulden Manor.

GLENARM CASTLE
Glenarm, Ballymena, Co. Antrim

The seat of the Earls of Antrim created in 1620 is haunted inside and outside. There has been a castle at Glenarm since the thirteenth-century when John Bisset was expelled from Scotland for murdering a rival during a tournament. He agreed to do penance by way of a pilgrimage to the Holy Land but instead he acquired pleasant lands hereabouts and built a castle. Today the old courthouse incorporates some of the original walls and an immured skeleton was discovered there in 1970. The present castle was built by Randle McDonnel, Knight Earl of Antrim, in 1636. In 1642 an invading Scots army burnt the castle and left it a ruin. In 1750 the 5th Earl of Antrim moved to Glenarm and employed an experienced English engineer, Christopher Myers, and he transformed the ruin into a Palladian mansion. Lord Antrim lived at the castle while work went on and one evening he entertained the local Presbyterian minister somewhat too well perhaps for on leaving the reverend gentleman fell over the half-built river wall to his death – one tragic event that may have some bearing on the psychic atmosphere and paranormal happenings in the gardens here over the years.

Among the ghosts here is that of a tall woman with a careworn face and deep-set eyes. She wears a skirt of blue and brown and her hands hold the long strings of a cap with frills such as Irish women once wore. She is usually seen standing in a doorway.

Another female apparition here also appears in a doorway and she was seen by a guest who was awakened very early in the morning by birds singing in the trees close to her window. It was already bright daylight and as the visitor turned on her elbow to reach for her water on the bedside table she saw, standing in the doorway looking at her, a woman, evidently a servant judging by her dress and just arisen, it would appear,

for she wore a mob cap and was holding the strings out in a dazed sort of way and her arms were bare. 'Well?' the surprised visitor asked, rather sharply, whereupon the figure vanished suddenly and completely.

This same ghost was reportedly seen over the years on many occasions, sometimes in the garden near a doorway, but usually indoors and always in the vicinity of a doorway as though about to enter and surprised at seeing someone there and unsure what to do next. Such a figure was certainly seen in 1990 and since then the same phantom form has appeared on a number of occasions to guests of Lord Dunluce. The woman appears to be solid and substantial and real in every way until she disappears with alarming rapidity. She is thought to have been a servant and is taken to be one by everyone who has seen her.

Once a visitor encountered this apparition as he approached the impressive entrance porch of Glenarm Castle and he nodded and asked if she knew whether Viscount Dunluce, the 14th Earl of Antrim, was at home. The 'servant' stared vacantly at the visitor for a second and then completely disappeared. 'One moment she was there,' I was told. 'The next – nothing. Quite incredible, and apparently scores of visitors have had the same experience'. But it does always seem to be visitors who encounter the ghost here and I am reminded of Paul Getty's remark to me when I asked whether he was alarmed by the stories of ghosts haunting his home and he replied that he was comforted by what he had been told by a friend in a similar position: that the ghosts never appeared to the owner, only to visitors.

One occupant of Glenarm Castle in 1997 told me there were definite parts of the castle that had an atmosphere, where there was a feeling that something was there that was not visible, and that something was about to happen, an air of expectancy that was only felt in certain areas; the corridor leading to the Blue Room and one place in the entrance hall being especially affected.

And then there was the garden. There, children in old-fashioned clothes have been seen at a distance, playing, but when the seer goes closer, the children suddenly disappear. It is almost as though they were visible from a certain distance and perhaps at a certain angle, and once that distance and angle is altered the 'vision' disappears. There have also been reports of a male figure in uniform or livery, suggesting a manservant, possibly a butler, groom or employee of some sort, who has also been encountered in the garden near the front porch of the house. He always seems to be in a hurry and has been seen disappearing up the steps and into the house or sometimes turning the corner of the castle and being lost to view – but always at considerable speed and often when it is raining. No one seems to know who this might be but it has been satisfactorily established that he is not a living person. Perhaps one day he will be in view long enough for a visitor to get a good description, maybe even a fleet-footed one may be quick enough to learn where he goes and/or why he is always in such a hurry.

JENKYN PLACE
Bentley, Hampshire

For some years, during the long occupancy of Gerald and Patricia Coke and their family of three sons and a daughter, the garden of Jenkyn Place, one of the oldest houses in the parish of Bentley in Hampshire, was regarded as one of the finest private gardens open to the public, 'beautifully designed and with a large collection of rare plants, roses and double herbaceous borders' as one guide puts it.

Gerald Edward Coke, a chairman of Glyndebourne Arts Trust, a director of the Royal Opera House, Covent Garden and a governor of the BBC, the only son of Major the Hon Sir John Coke, lived with his family for fifty years at justly famous Jenkyn Place: famous for its history, its beauty and its ghosts. When I took some Ghost Club Society members to Jenkyn Place he met us, showed us round the house and garden and talked to us of ghosts.

There had been a building on this site for centuries and probably long before 1687 when Robert and Ann Lutman built the farmhouse that forms the core of the present building. Much altered by various owners over the years, the Cokes reduced the house to what it might have been – a small country house of about the turn of the seventeenth century.

In the garden is Jancknes's Well which is mentioned in the Domesday Book, the record of William I's survey of England in 1086. Gerald Coke told us Jancknes means the son of Janck, or Jack or John and so is really the same as Johnson or Jackson and all similar surnames. The Pilgrim's Way, which led by the shortest route from church to church from Winchester to Canterbury, passed over what is now the front drive of the house on its way from Froyle church to Bentley church and the pilgrims invariably paused, it is said, to drink at the well and to throw in a coin for luck.

Long before the Cokes went to Jenkyn Place in 1941, during the occupancy of the Lawsons in fact, back in the 1920s, the haunting of the garden seems to have been well established – and varied. There are many stories of an unidentified White Lady frequently being seen in the vicinity of the little bridge over the nearby lane and this often reported appearance is well remembered by some of the villagers today. I recall Ann Gordon telling me that she and a friend were the only people at Jenkyn Place one evening, apart from the Cokes, when they both saw a tall woman in a long white dress glide smoothly across the well-tended lawn and disappear in the direction of the white bridge. They thought there must be another guest they had not met but when they saw no one later on they asked Patricia Coke about the lady in white and learned, for the first time, about the apparitional White Lady.

The only ghost story they had previously heard pertaining to Jenkyn Place was the redoubtable 'Mrs Waggs'. This was the name given to the incessant phantom that has long haunted Jenkyn Place, although who she actually was nobody seems to know. Perhaps she was a former housekeeper or possibly a children's nurse who became

inordinately attached to the beautiful house; there must have been many such people in the long history of Jenkyn Place.

Among the witnesses for ghosts at Jenkyn Place was Micky Joy who lived nearby. Michael Joy CMG, MC, formerly with HM Diplomatic Service, educated at Winchester and New College, Oxford, held diplomatic posts in Saigon, Washington, Addis Ababa and Stockholm and was not the type of person to be misled or easily deceived, yet he told me he undoubtedly saw the ghostly 'Mrs Waggs'. Apart from appearances in various parts of the garden 'Mrs Waggs' was frequently seen, especially during the winter months, in the hall (significantly perhaps one the oldest parts of the house), on the stairs that run up the west side of the house and in an upstairs room.

There is a tradition that the figure disappears into a second room at the head of the stairs, picks up a lighted candle, and then continues her tour of the house and sometimes the garden. The bedroom which the ghost reputedly visits has three heart-shaped pieces of wood inserted into the flooring to replace knots in the wood while a formidable iron bar on the inside of the door looks as though it could hold the door fast against anything in this world, but whether these features have any connection with the ghost or the haunting is not known. It was pointed out to me that the bar is ingeniously constructed and there was once a rope running to the wall by the bed so that the door could be fastened as required by someone while they were in bed . . .

Micky Joy told me that one wintry day in the early part of the Second World War when Jenkyn Place was empty, he and his mother, an aunt and two of his sisters were shown over the house by a caretaker. Micky Joy, his aunt and one of his sisters had

remained in one of the downstairs rooms while his mother and the other sister were taken off by the caretaker to another part of the house.

After a little while Micky and his two companions thought they had better join the others but they did not know where the caretaker had gone. They stood in the hall and, noticing a movement at the top of the stairs, were somewhat surprised to see the figure of a woman crossing the landing near the top of the stairs. As they watched she turned and walked away from them and disappeared through an open door. Naturally they thought they had seen the caretaker and they hastily climbed the stairs, but when they reached the top they heard the caretaker's voice downstairs and they turned to see her appear with old Mrs Joy and one of her daughters. They then established that there was nobody other than themselves upstairs and nobody else in the house at the time. The aunt, Miss Phyllis Joy, described the figure as 'a little old woman in black'.

Years later, during an evening visit with the Cokes, Micky Joy and one of his daughters were in the garden when, as they turned the corner of a tall green and copper-beech hedge where a pair of eighteenth-century lions guarded the entrance to the walk that led to the Italian 'Sleeping Lion', they both saw a woman moving hurriedly across the lawn ahead of them – and Micky immediately recognised the woman he had seen at the top of the stairs during the family visit. 'There was no doubt about it,' he told me. 'It was Mrs Waggs all right – she haunts the garden as well as the house . . .'

After Micky's death his widow Ann wrote to me: 'Micky was fascinated by the idea of ghosts at Marelands [where he lived], Jenkyn Place and other old houses he'd known. He was so sceptical about all sorts of things that it always surprised me that he should be interested in ghosts and often quote from several books of yours we have in the house . . .' Personal experience makes all the difference!

110

Others who have had odd experiences in the garden at Jenkyn Place include proffressional concert singer Dorothea St Hill Bourne who saw a woman in a white dress walking across the lawn as she sat having tea with Patricia Coke one afternoon. It looked like rain and Dorothea told me she joked to Patricia Coke that the poor woman would get drenched if she wasn't careful whereupon Patricia spun round to see what her friend was talking about but by that time the figure had completely disappeared. 'She was as large as life,' Dorothea said. 'The next moment she simply wasn't there!'

Patricia Coke told me that a few days before she had been sitting in exactly the same place in the garden when she heard the distinct grind of wheels as some vehicle drew up at the front of the house and she got up to see if it was the person she was expecting – there was nothing there, no person, no vehicle and no explanation for the sounds she had heard. There has long been a tradition that a phantom coach and horses pulls into the drive of Jenkyn Place and I talked with a former employee at Jenkyn Place who well recalled more than one reliable person who claimed to have seen the phantom coach: one was my informant's own brother who, more than fifty years later, still maintained that he had heard and seen the remarkable phenomenon and that there was no natural explanation that could have accounted for the experience. One wonders whether the visual aspect of this phantasm has now run out, almost like a battery running down, and now all that is left are the sounds; perhaps these too will cease before many more years have passed.

Visitors often mentioned a lady in a white dress, Dorothea was told, whom they had seen in the garden; on cold days they thought it might be an eccentric family member and were worried about her catching cold: they were dumbfounded when they learned that they had probably seen one of the family ghosts! Quite often too, Patricia Coke told Dorothea St Hill Bourne, people came back to the house having had a walk round the garden and they asked about the figure they had seen: someone who looked like a housekeeper in a mobcap.

On the south side of the house one of Gerald Coke's sons saw a female figure when he was a boy of six or seven. He was very shaken by the experience and told his mother that he had seen a woman dressed like a housekeeper. On occasions the same boy would complain of a strange female figure passing through his bedroom at night.

On the west side of the house there is a charming little bedroom with a view of the garden. Once when this delightful room was allocated to a sensible eighteen-year-old friend of the family during her visit to Jenkyn Place, after one night she refused to sleep in the room again, saying she could not possibly spend another night there. Subsequently it transpired that she had seen 'something' in the garden that caused her to make her irrevocable decision.

Some years ago John Christie, founder of the Glyndebourne Festival and holder of the rare Military Cross – he was a wealthy landowner whose family had owned Glyndebourne for 700 years – was visiting Jenkyn Place. Gerald Coke was at that time chairman of Glyndebourne Arts Trust and the two men were taking tea in the upstairs sitting room when Christie suddenly remarked upon the fact that Gerald's housekeeper had been standing staring at them for several minutes before disappearing into a solid wall! At the time Christie had never heard of the reputed ghost of 'Mrs Waggs' or any other ghost at Jenkyn Place. Next morning he came hurriedly in from a walk in the garden to say he had just seen the same figure and she had disappeared into a hedge!

There seems no doubt that a figure suggesting a housekeeper or servant of some kind has been seen at Jenkyn Place for many years. Visitors and local people and one resident family all say she is dressed in a fitting mobcap, a brown dress, and a white apron with the ends turned up; several witnesses find the figure reminiscent of the Jane Austen period.

Looking back I recall so well summer visits to that exceptionally beautiful garden and especially the occasion when members of The Ghost Club Society toured the house and garden and the sombre voice of Gerald Coke saying, modestly, 'I suppose you could call this a haunted house – and it certainly has a haunted garden!'

One spring day I had the idea of a party of Ghost Club Society members spending a night or several nights inside Jenkyn Place and in the ghost-ridden garden in a concerted effort to explore the mystery of the persistent ghosts that have haunted Jenkyn Place for so long and have been seen by so many people but in response to my enquiry Gerald Coke said: 'We would be delighted to help with your investigations but 'Mrs Waggs' only seems to appear in February and if you want to come and meet her during that month, do let me know . . .' Sadly, due to circumstances beyond my control, including security problems, this proved impossible and with the death of Gerald Coke and later of Patricia Coke and then the change of ownership of Jenkyn Place, that unique opportunity passed.

LAMB HOUSE
Rye, East Sussex

I can't help wondering whether the ghosts here have anything to do with the unhappy tenants of this interesting house. One of the National Trust's most prized small houses, the occupants change with some frequency, in 1996 the new occupants leaving after less than two months.

This dreamy, Georgian red-brick house has an acre of haunted gardens surrounded by a high wall and altogether the property would seem to be ideal for the right people:

the tenants have eight private rooms, three bathrooms and a good view of the town. However, there are substantial problems in running such a house for the National Trust, financial and practical, and there is also the task of dealing with visitors twice a week, shepherding parties from room to room, answering difficult literary questions and endlessly polishing sticky finger marks from displays – not to mention the ghosts. It has been called 'a house to chill the blood'.

Lamb House was originally the home of James Lamb, thirteen times Mayor of Rye, a loyal royalist who, when he heard that King George I, returning from one of his frequent visits to his beloved Hanover, had been caught in a storm and driven onto nearby Camber Sands, immediately left his heavily pregnant wife and rode out that wild and windy night to meet the King and offer him the hospitality of his house. He even gave up his own bedroom for the royal guest who stayed four nights and acted as godfather to one of Mrs Martha Lamb's sons (she had nine children) who was born the night the King arrived and who was, of course, named George.

Three years later Mayor James Lamb narrowly escaped death when his brother-in-law, Allan Grebell, to whom Lamb had loaned his cloak, was murdered in nearby Rye churchyard by a paranoid butcher named Breads who thought he was attacking the Mayor of Rye. Breads was duly hanged for murder on the Salts outside the Landgate and his body suspended from a gibbet nearby, at a spot still known as Gibbet's Marsh – and the ghost of Allan Grebell is said to have haunted Lamb House and its garden ever since.

Novelist and short story writer, Henry James's poignant ghost story *The Turn of the Screw* is a masterpiece that has had echoes here down the years although the story was not actually written here, unlike some of the author's famous works including *The Golden Bowl*, *The Ambassadors* and *The Wings of a Dove*, which were conceived and written at Lamb House. Born in New York of a wealthy father in 1843, he became naturalised as a British subject in 1915, received the Order of Merit in 1916 and died shortly afterwards at Chelsea; he never married. Among the unexplained happenings he experienced during his occupancy of Lamb House from 1897 until 1916 were mysterious fires that were discovered in odd parts of the property and one that occurred within a year of his moving in was potentially disastrous and it took the local fire brigade more than three hours to extinguish.

During Henry James's golden years at Lamb House he entertained many distinguished visitors – most of them no strangers to ghosts – including H. G. Wells, Max Beerbohm, Hilaire Belloc, G. K. Chesterton, George Gissing, Joseph Conrad, Stephen Crane, Fort Madox Brown, Edmund Gosse, Rudyard Kipling (who was always very aware of the paranormal and had a mediumistic sister), Edith Wharton, Compton Mackenzie and Hugh Walpole, many of whom wrote about psychic activity in a sensitive and convincing manner. Portraits of King George I, Joseph Conrad, G. K. Chesterton, Hilaire Belloc, George Gissing and Rudyard Kipling now grace the hall at Lamb House together with several fine portraits of Henry James himself.

Henry James was followed at Lamb House by the Benson brothers, E. F. Benson, the novelist, and A. C. Benson, Master of Magdalen College, Oxford. The brothers did not

get on with each other so E.F. lived at the house in term time and went abroad during the college vacations, leaving it to A. C., author of the poem 'Land of Hope and Glory'.

Viola Bayley, whose home was opposite Lamb House, has recalled appearing before E. F. Benson in his capacity as magistrate. Then a shy seventeen-year-old, she had been charged with illegal parking – something that is still all too easy in Rye. 'It was raining and the gallery was full,' she recalled, 'and he played to it, asking me if I had any previous convictions . . . I felt awful.' Later that same day E. F. Benson went over to take tea with the Bayley family and said to Viola: 'We had rather a lot of fun this morning, didn't we?' 'I could have killed him' Viola Bayley recalled.

E. F. Benson was always interested in psychic phenomena (as H. Montgomery Hyde reveals in his *Story of Lamb House*, 1966) and he recounted several personal experiences while he lived at Lamb House, including witnessing the famed apparition of the murdered Allan Grebell. E. F. Benson used Lamb House as the setting for his popular *Mapp and Lucia* novels.

One summer's day E. F. Benson was sitting in the garden with the vicar of Rye, facing the garden wall, when he saw the figure of a man walk past. 'He was dressed in black and wore a cape over his shoulders,' he said afterwards. 'His head was turned away and he vanished after walking a couple of steps.' The vicar saw him too and jumped up, exclaiming, 'Who on earth is that?' They looked all round the garden and in the Secret Garden beyond the wall but there was no sign of the figure they had both clearly seen. There was no way out of the Secret Garden, which was completely enclosed with high walls.

On another occasion, during the course of a séance held in the Garden Room (demolished by a direct hit in the Second World War), the medium, just before she went into the trance state, pointed to an empty mahogany and cane chair and asked, 'Who is the man in a cloak sitting in that chair?' The story goes that it was the actual chair in which the dead body of Allan Grebell had been discovered. After being attacked he had staggered out of the churchyard and had managed the short distance to his own home, opposite Lamb House, and had there collapsed in the chair and bled to death. Subsequently James Lamb was given the chair 'as a souvenir of the tragedy'. According to E. F. Benson the medium had never heard of the Grebell murder.

Rumer Godden, author of more than fifty books and a two-volume autobiography, lived at Lamb House with her husband James for a time in the 1970s and during their first few weeks in the house, she told me, they experienced poltergeist activity, especially in the dark, airless and old-fashioned kitchen. They raised the flooring, knocked down the back wall and made the room sunny and light but the disturbances continued. The new boiler burst, new pipes burst almost as soon as they were installed, saucepans flew off shelves, electricity fused. The Goddens asked a priest to come and bless the house. He came and for a while things improved.

During Rumer Godden's time at Lamb House the place was alive with children – her own grandchildren and their friends and this seemed to promote an atmosphere in which Rumer distinctly sensed, and perhaps saw, the two children so splendidly portrayed in The Turn of the Screw, Flora and Miles, although the immortal tale that has been called 'the most terrifying short story in English literature' was not written at

Lamb House and in fact there had been no children living at the house for 200 years. James and Martha Lamb had had nine children and no doubt their descendents had children too but the last Lamb, Augustus, was a celibate clergyman. After his death the house was bought by a Mr Bellingham who had no children; Henry James followed and then the Bensons – all bachelors. An elderly lady, Mrs Fullerton, was next and then an elderly Montgomery Hyde followed by an equally mature Rumer and James Godden. Delightful and perceptive Rumer Godden told me, 'I do have a penchant for attracting the unusual and peculiar.' At Rye she wrote in Henry James's study and she would often hear children's voices. There were no children in the house at the time but she 'knew they were the voices of Miles and Flora – the creepy little pair in The Turn of the Screw; E. F. Benson heard them too'.

Could it be that in some odd way the essence of the two ghost children, Flora and Miles, so influenced Henry James that they returned when real children were visiting the house? Rumer Godden explains it in A House with Four Walls (1989) like this:

> Now suddenly Lamb House was alive with those shrill, sometimes piercing child voices, scampering of feet – thumping of feet. There was sliding down the banisters, toys left on the stairs, a new untidiness, a quickening of life and, sometime, in the hurdy-gurdy I had a strange sense of 'presences', two other children, silent, well-behaved. It was as if they were watching. Soon I knew who they were, Miles and Flora. Our own children had brought them out of the Green Study where Henry James had conceived them. After our four had gone I had the feeling that Miles and Flora were still there.

Writing about a visit to Lamb House in 1997 Christopher Hart refers to the dining-room as 'harbouring dark secrets' and to stepping through French windows into the garden . . . 'beautifully maintained and little changed since James's day. There are flaking, ochre brick walls, smooth lawns, flowerbeds, wisteria, a trellis covered in roses and a venerable mulberry tree. But above all, there is silence – no sound of traffic at all, though we are in the middle of Rye . . . There is a ghost in this garden: a room. James actually did most of his writing in the Garden Room . . . and one can still trace the outline of foundation bricks in the south lawn.'

And then comes the admission – or is it merely journalistic licence? Judge for yourselves. 'There are other wraiths here,' writes Christopher Hart. 'Looking out across the lawn to the shadowy trees beyond, I swear I caught a glimpse of Miles, standing in the moonlight, staring up at his governess looking out of the old tower. And lurking in wait for them, the evil Miss Jessel, "dark as midnight in her black dress, her haggard beauty and her unutterable woe." And suddenly, despite the warm sunlight on this golden autumn day, I shivered a little and looked about me . . .'

For me a lasting memory of one visit to Lamb House at Rye is sitting with Charles de Salis on the seat in the garden, facing the bricked-up doorway to the Secret Garden where E. F. Benson and the vicar of Rye were sitting when they saw the ghost of a murdered man; sadly he did not manifest for us.

Human testimony proves that something of the past lingers still in this beautiful house and garden; sometimes, it would appear from the trail of unhappy tenants, it becomes too active for comfort.

The Lost Gardens of Heligan
Pentewan, St Austell, Cornwall

The Lost Gardens of Heligan, near the picturesque village of Mevagissey in Cornwall, are haunted as they should be. This award-winning fifty acres of superb and magical complex of four walled gardens and a kitchen garden have been restored to their former glory as a living museum of nineteenth-century horticulture.

Here you may encounter a shade from the past in the Italian Garden, the Ravine, the Crystal Grotto or in any of the summerhouses or on the Rides and Lawns all surrounded by rare and beautiful shrubs, in fact almost anywhere in this sleeping beauty of a garden, lost for more than seventy years under a mountain of bramble, ivy and rampant laurel and brought back to life largely through the untiring efforts of archaeologist Tim Smit who believed restoration was possible and with the help and support and encouragement of John Nelson, a restorer of ancient buildings and John Willis who had just inherited the estate.

The regeneration of these gardens is a remarkable story for in less than five years a 200-year-old masterpiece of a garden has been brought back to life after three-quarters of a century of neglect. With the help of a few old photographs and tithe maps the original paths have been located together with such treasures as the Paxtonian Vinery and everything has been restored as closely as possible to the original plan. During the course of extended study of the fading photographs and excavation and exploration, the story emerged of a haunted garden.

In his *Lost Gardens of Heligan* (Gollancz, 1997) Tim Smit says 'there have been many strange experiences at Heligan . . . which have been relayed to me by those I trust . . .' and he goes on to reveal that stories of sightings of a ghostly Grey Lady were common when the gardens were extant; in fact that part of a ride between the house and the shelter woodlands is often referred to on old maps as the Grey Lady's Walk. This ghost 'is said to be regularly seen walking away from the house'. An elderly resident of Mevagissey told Tim that once when she had seen the apparition, she followed it into the trees where it disappeared.

In his book, in a chapter entitled 'In the Shadows' Tim reveals that the demands placed on them and the sheer exhaustion of many of the working team, created tensions that surfaced from time to time and when the pressure was really beginning to tell on everyone and the general feeling of tetchiness was replaced by a black mood that seemed to permeate all their lives, Tim realised that something might be deeply wrong; and the backcloth to it all was a series of unexplained events. While each individual episode could have been laughed off as a single event, as so often happens in these cases, the steady accumulation of bizarre happenings dented the healthiest of scepticism.

Tim says at the time he neither believed nor disbelieved in ghosts and other paranormal phenomena but his grandmother, whose home was Hartford Hall, where he often stayed as a child, was among those who regarded the place as haunted; indeed Tim's grandmother talked to her 'ghosts' as if they were old friends and once she told him she had seen the figure of a monk leaning over his bed. Now, all these years later, in the light of what was happening and being experienced by the whole team, he began to think again about those stories of ghosts and ghostly happenings and he began to hear some very strange tales of odd occurrences at Heligan.

In 1978 an Australian plumber working on conservations in Heligan House, discovered the then overgrown Melon Garden and decided to camp there. He collected some rubbish and wood and proceeded to build himself a fire inside the ruins of the two-storey building but, try as he might, he could not light a fire – then suddenly the whole pile burst into flames which shot high into the night sky where he watched them form the distinct and clear shape of a cross. As suddenly as it had started the fire died, leaving only a pile of cold ash . . . Terrified, the hard-headed Aussie fled back to the house where, wide-eyed, he explained what had happened, collected his things, hurriedly packed his bags and left, never to be seen again.

This all sounded to Tim like a classic hair-raising story such as he would have enjoyed in his teenage years but after the gardens were opened to the public he began to receive a steady stream of letters and telephone calls from visitors relating equally extraordinary stories of personal experiences in the gardens; some of which were seemingly incapable of any rational explanation. And it didn't end there.

Individual visitors were often convinced that in the gardens they were accompanied by their late husbands or wives – for hours on end, as they lost themselves in the atmosphere of the place. Others described in detail feelings of being 'not alone', of invisible presences, in the area of the Rockery and, in the region of the Wishing Well, there were consistent reports from visitors who claimed they saw someone walk through the wall of the Crystal Grotto. Psychically-attuned visitors talked of a tragic couple who met secretly in the Grotto and of the dark and gloomy moods experienced there. It is said to be haunted by an elemental.

As time passed chats with the old head gardener and others in the Melon Garden did nothing to ease the atmosphere of unease that pervaded much of the garden and affected everyone. People talked openly about 'the spooks in the garden' and no one felt comfortable being alone while locking up the gardens at night. Unexplained footsteps seemed to be everywhere but especially it seemed in the old fruit store; one of the seedmen complained that his seeds were continually moved, even out of locked rooms, and there was never any explanation.

One evening a couple stopped Tim and asked whether the gardens were haunted. As he hesitated to give a non-committal reply, they said that the previous week, while alone in the Melon Garden, they had gone into the dark house, under the fruit store, where all the forcing pots are stored in a row and they described how they both watched, transfixed, as the pot lids lifted by themselves, one by one, as though someone invisible was going down the line checking on the crops inside. After the last lid was released they heard a deep sigh and then all went quiet and the atmosphere noticeably warmed up and improved.

Later, when the restoration of the Flower Garden was proceeding to schedule, the sense that 'something' was frequently present and that the workmen were not in control of their own destinies grew stronger and stronger. Tim tells me he had never felt out of his depth in that way before in his whole life. One day he found a friend and fellow-worker, who had been collecting ferns for an exhibition, white-faced and shaking. He had been working on the Tump, among the ancient beeches and timeless holly trees where, uncharacteristically, his dog, Fly, her hackles raised, had refused to join him. Alone among the trees and bushes of long, long ago he suddenly became aware of someone or something near him. He felt the hairs on the back of his neck erect and as he stood up he saw, to his horror, an enormous black shape emerge out of nowhere and slowly drift out of the trees. This was in broad daylight and whatever it was appeared and disappeared in circumstances that defy explanation.

Things became so difficult that, as a last resort, Tim invited a vicar to come to Heligan and he was pleasantly surprised to find the man of the cloth took the subject of ghosts very seriously. They toured the various locations where 'activity' had been at its height – the most haunted places if you like – and ended up at the Tump. Here the vicar grew very intense and said he felt that particular part of the gardens had an association with evil. As they walked back the vicar said he felt he needed special advice from his bishop and he spoke of disturbing cases of possession of which he had personal experience, of speaking in strange tongues and voices that changed from a bass growl to a high-pitched whine and he talked of ghosts as spirits in need of release 'after missing the boat to the afterlife'. He said there were often ghosts at places of great sadness or tragedy and some human beings and many animals were acutely sensitive to their presence.

The vicar returned when he had taken advice and he was prepared to conduct exorcisms at identified locations. Accordingly they visited the Mount, the Crystal Grotto, the Wishing Well, the Melon Garden and finally the Tump. As Tim Smit says, 'With a new season around the corner we hoped that the whole garden would now be at peace with itself. All we could do was to wait'.

I have to say that I have recently received a number of letters from people who have experienced 'odd' happenings in various parts of this haunted garden, especially the Lost Valley where a strange and unexplained 'deathly stillness' and complete absence of bird song is frequently remarked upon and then there are the voices, unexplained human and inhuman figures, the mystifying sounds and smells and the overall sense of something not of this world. The glorious Lost Gardens of Heligan are indeed haunted for many people lucky enough to visit this unique place.

MARKYATE CELL
Markyate, St Albans, Hertfordshire

Some thirty years ago I wrote to Mr S. A. Sursham, at that time the elderly owner of wonderful Markyate Cell, situated in the tiny hamlet of Markyate, near St Albans. Twenty years before that I had heard all about the legends and ghost stories long associated with that singular house and rambling garden; of the seventeenth-century occupant, a young and attractive woman – unhappily married – who dressed as a highwayman and terrorised the surrounding countryside. Long after her death she would be heard and seen, it was said, riding down the drive on her coal-black horse or staggering through the garden, mortally wounded, as she dragged herself back to the secret room in her home, only to expire outside the hidden entrance . . .

The name of Markyate Cell is derived from the hermitage built there by Roger, a monk of St Albans, early in the twelfth century. It was after Roger had been on a pilgrimage to Jerusalem that he settled as a hermit at Markyate, under the care of the then Abbot of St Albans. There have long been persistent stories of a subterranean passage linking Markyate Cell with St Albans Abbey (some four miles distant) and that in this underground retreat 'the restless spirits of departed monks patter and shuffle in the dead of night' (according to a newspaper correspondent of 1892).

Roger died about 1122 and was buried in St Albans Abbey, where his shrine was visited by King Henry III in 1257. In 1118, when her wealthy parents attempted to force her into a marriage against her will, Christina, a member of an Anglo-Saxon family in Huntingdonshire, fled to Markyate to become one of Roger's hermits. It was feared that, if he discovered her whereabouts, the Bishop of Lincoln might intervene, so Christina's presence at Markyate was kept a close secret, and we learn that she was voluntarily enclosed in a cell measuring only one span and a half where for four years she sat on hard stone (there being insufficient room to stand) suffering extremes of temperature, hunger and thirst. Under these rigorous conditions she seems to have acquired, apart from various physical ailments(!), a great reputation for sanctity and in due course she succeeded Roger as head of the hermitage. Christina was also renowned for her fine hand-embroidery and in 1155 samples of her work were sent to Pope

Adrian IV. The priory at Markyate remained until the dissolution of the monasteries in the sixteenth century, when much of the building was pulled down but some of the old material was incorporated in the new mansion built by Humphrey Bourchier, Chancellor of the Exchequer and Master of the King's Pastimes – the latter probably quite an interesting post when the monarch was Henry VIII! After Bourchier's death, his widow, Elizabeth, married George Ferrers in 1541 and much of their Tudor house is still evident, despite extensive alterations in the nineteenth century. One can still discern the general Tudor form of the house; many of the windows are Tudor too and much of the actual stonework, while the haunted garden, still and strangely peaceful, almost a place apart, is laid out in perfect Tudor style.

During the seventeenth century the lady of the house was a certain Catherine Ferrers, known as 'the wicked Lady Ferrers'; she had been married at the age of thirteen to a member of the aristocracy named Fanshawe, but the marriage was not a success. It may have been the disillusionment of an unhappy marriage or perhaps it was loneliness and frustration that first caused Catherine Ferrers to turn to crime, but there is little doubt that it was the danger and excitement and not the financial rewards that gratified her when she changed into a highwayman's costume and practised the art of 'stand-and-deliver' throughout the countryside thereabouts. A secret room was built into the kitchen chimney, reached by a concealed stairway and there she stored the three-cornered hat, the mask, the buckskin breeches and

the riding-cloak and it was down this secret stairway (which I examined) that she would steal to mount her coal-black horse and ride wildly down the drive and away to lonely coach routes to hold up, and shoot without argument it has to be said, travellers on their journeys north and south. For years she carried on the subterfuge and the coachmen and their passengers only breathed easier once they left behind them the leafy lanes of Hertfordshire.

Then one night on nearby No Man's Land Common there was an argument, an exchange of shots in the dark night, and Lady Ferrers, although wounded, managed to escape from the travellers she had sought to rob and struggling home, she fell off her horse, staggered into the house and reached the door to her secret staircase but there she collapsed and expired. Next morning her body was found and although the secret was out, the doorway was bricked up and remained so for well over a hundred years.

Shortly after the funeral, with her faithful black horse following, stories began to circulate in the surrounding countryside that her ghost had been seen abroad; some said she was seen riding hell-for-leather on horseback down the drive, others declared that they had seen her spectral figure by an old oak tree in the garden, under which she is thought to have buried the proceeds of her robberies – which have never been found; while still others have reported seeing the slim figure of a 'highwayman' riding a black horse at nearby No Man's Land and in shady lanes thereabouts. Concerning the highwayman's treasure an old rhyme is still well-known in the district that runs: 'Near the Cell there is a Well. Near the Well there is a Tree. And under the Tree the Treasure be.' Although there is now no trace of a well in the grounds of Markyate Cell a wellhead was shown to me near the outer wall and presumably where there is a wellhead there was once a well. Incidentally the house was once owned and occupied by Sir Thomas Beecham who may well have brought the wellhead over from Italy.

An older legend is that the treasure was confiscated by the nuns of St Trinity who buried it at the Reformation – and this age old story may account for the fact that over the centuries the ghosts of nuns have been reported wandering silently in the garden of Markyate Cell.

When Glanville Squiers was researching his monumental *Secret Hiding Places* (published in 1934) he visited Markyate Cell only to be told that details of the famous 'highwayman's hiding place' had been lost; however he did establish that several curious and grim finds had been made in the grounds at different times. Apart from coffined remains, skulls and bones had been unearthed as well as the skeletons of a human being and a horse. A small find of ancient coins was also made, quite recently he was told, although no details were made available to him. He told me he also learned of the stories of buried treasure, of ghostly forms being seen in the garden and about a long-lost underground passage.

There was a bad fire at Markyate Cell in 1841 and some of the men who worked to put out the blaze maintained that they saw the ghostly form of Lady Ferrers. When the fire was eventually extinguished Mr Adey, the owner at that time, decided to open the mysterious bricked-up doorway; but he encountered great difficulty in enlisting men for the work locally, for it was common knowledge that the house and garden were haunted and that apart from the ghost of the wicked Lady Ferrers unaccountable sighs and groans and other noises were frequently heard. At length workmen from London broke down the brickwork and opened the doorway. They found that the narrow stone stairway led up to a heavy oak door which they broke through, only to find afterwards that the door opened by means of a concealed spring. The room, however, yielded no secrets, only many spiders and bats.

There does seem to be overwhelming evidence that the ghost of Catherine Ferrers has been seen here; either riding her swift black horse; or in the vicinity of a particular tree; or standing, still and silent at various spots in the garden (once she was seen by a number of people at a parish tea and Mr Sursham's daughter once saw an unexplained woman who disappeared); or in the kitchen or other parts of this interesting house.

I found Mr E. A. Sursham utterly delightful. He readily agreed to my visiting and exploring the house and garden, which I did on my own, with my wife, with my son Chris who took photographs, and with a group of Ghost Club Society members. Sursham told me of his long life at Markyate Cell and his conviction that the place was indeed haunted – although not in any unpleasant way – and the garden and drive had been the scene of spectral visitors on numerous occasions. Sometimes the spectre, usually that of a youngish female, was seen by several people at the same time and it seemed most common during the late afternoon or early evening. There were plenty of occasions when friends or acquaintances of Mr Sursham visited Markyate Cell for the first time, knowing nothing of any ghostly manifestations, and they would ask about the female they had seen for a moment in the garden and seemed to disappear mysteriously when they approached.

There is no doubt that the haunting is a long-standing one for early historians of Hertfordshire such as William Gerish, were researching and writing about the ghosts at Markyate Cell and elsewhere more than a hundred years ago. Stories such as the one that on occasions the phantom form of Catherine Ferrers was seen swinging aimlessly on the branches of a tree take on credence when we learn that on occasions she would climb up into a tree with branches overhanging the road, and drop down on her unsuspecting victim, a passing traveller.

Gerish maintained that ghostly sights and sounds were to be encountered on the nearby Dunstable Road, north as far as Gustard Wood and in several roads and lanes in the vicinity of St Albans.

Christina Hole, that 'careful, thorough and completely unbiased' acknowledged authority on English ghost lore and one time president of The Folklore Society, stated in her excellent *Haunted England* (Batsford, 1940) as she related to me personally that Markyate Cell 'was long haunted and perhaps still is, by the ghost of the "wicked" Lady Ferrers'. She may well have published such a statement, for Christina Hole told me she found Markyate Cell to be the most fascinating of all the haunted houses she had visited and it possessed the one haunted garden where she thought she had herself caught sight of the ghostly Lady Ferrers. Christina had been walking in the garden, accompanied by the owner, when they both saw the figure of a young woman at the far end of the garden. She appeared to be dressed in very out-of-date clothes but before Christina or her companion could really note very much the figure simply disappeared. The owner told her he had seen the same form or figure once before, in the same place, at about the same time in the afternoon, and just as briefly.

Long standing Ghost Club Society member Tony Broughall in his unpublished manuscript *Ghosts of Bedfordshire and Hertfordshire* (compiled in 1978) reveals that around 1900 a gamekeeper saw the mounted ghost of Lady Ferrers, disguised as a highwayman, riding along the A5 road towards Dunstable and he took the opportunity to fire his rifle at her without it having any effect whatsoever; and in the summer of 1901 and again in the early 1960s her ghost was seen in the garden, one of the witnesses for the latter sightings being the daughter of Mr Sursham. In December 1970 the manager of a nearby public house, exercising his dog at 11.30 p.m. one evening, heard the sound of a galloping horse approaching. The perpetrator of the sounds seemed to pass close by – so close in fact that he said afterwards that he believed he could have touched the horse – but he saw nothing and not a bush or shrub or blade of grass moved although his dog was distinctly affected and required considerable reassurance and comfort before he would resume his walk.

The public house manager referred to was employed at The Wicked Lady, a memorial to a singular ghost, situated on No Man's Land Common where Lady Ferrers is thought to have been mortally wounded and a public house (then under a different name) that was reputedly used by rogues and vagabonds in the days when Lady Ferrers was terrorising the neighbourhood. The Wicked Lady, which I may say from personal knowledge, is a hostelry of character and charm providing excellent nourishment, is itself haunted by the sound of a woman sobbing and this phenomenon too is attributed to the wicked Lady Ferrers.

OLD ABBEY HOUSE
Barnwell, Cambridge

At a Society for Psychical Research gathering, back in the 1950s, I talked with Professor F. J. M. Stratton (president of that society from 1953 to 1955) about the ghosts of Abbey House, a case he followed for many years recording the protracted haunting of which he had personal knowledge since he rented the house for a while and resided there. In fact this noted astronomer was fascinated by the stories of ghostly activity centred around his house and garden for something like forty years. After his death in 1961 he passed his bulky file on this outstanding haunted house to the Society for Psychical Research.

The Abbey House, in Abbey Road off the Newmarket Road, was built about 1580 from the remnants of Barnwell Priory that stood nearby, a twelfth-century religious foundation that once housed thirty Augustinian canons. Said to have had a church 200 feet long, the priory profoundly influenced life in Cambridge during the Middle Ages. A house of Benedictine nuns was established in what is now Jesus Lane and the nuns of St Radegund built a large church which serves in part as the beautiful chapel of Jesus College. Barnwell Priory, the oldest and most wealthy of the religious houses in Cambridge, surrendered to the University and the King in 1538 when the houses of the friars were dissolved.

In 1714 Jacob 'Squire' Butler, a famous Cambridge character, inherited the abbey estate. Six feet four inches tall, a graduate who became a barrister and who engaged in numerous lawsuits, he called himself 'Old Briton' in his old age because of his many strenuous fights for what he considered to be his rights. Once, in an attempt to re-establish the ancient custom that decreed that anything still standing on the age-old fairground on 24 August could be trampled down by stall-holders and that booths not cleared away by Michaelmas Day could be demolished, he drove his carriage through piles of crockery. Among his other eccentricities, long before his death at the age of eighty-four in 1765, 'Squire' Butler had an enormous oak coffin made for himself, and at his funeral this coffin was lowered into a vault and a smaller, leaded coffin, containing his body, placed inside it. But all this does not seem to have prevented his ghost from walking in the garden.

Some years ago there were repeated reports of the appearance of the unmistakable form of 'Squire' Butler, who died in the house. Those who encountered the tall, fierce-looking figure, learned from Jimmy Westworth Day, that renowned raconteur, author and collector of ghostly happenings, of the dark-green wool coat with gold-braid edges, and from independent and separate but corroborating reports a picture has emerged of a lanky, overbearing figure in green thigh-length coat with gold buttons and heavy cuffs, a satin embroidered waistcoat, green wool breeches and black leather shoes with metal buckles. On his head he wore a black felt tricorn hat with gold-braid edge and he sported a long, thin cane walking-stick. Such a figure was apparently encountered many times in and about the old gabled house he knew so well,

There is also a well-authenticated Grey Lady ghost, sometimes referred to as a lady in a grey cloak; she is believed to have been one of the nuns of St Radegund who came to the abbey to meet her lover, an Austin friar. Her ghost, a hesitant figure, was usually seen in the area of the tall iron gates set in the grey stone wall and on the age-old path at the back of the house, amid the mouldering stones of the vanished abbey. She was reportedly seen once in 1968, twice in 1969 and once in 1986.

This striking phenomenon seems to have been especially prevalent during the occupation of the Lawson family, between 1903 and 1911. All the family, servants and sometimes visitors claimed to see the female form in the garden. She was dressed in a darkish robe or it could well have been a nun's habit. Her features were never seen distinctly but her general appearance and carriage suggested an age of about thirty. She seems always to have been encountered during the hours of darkness and often between midnight and 4.00 a.m., sometimes inside the house. She was reportedly seen most frequently during the months of February and March, seemingly three or four times a month for a time.

The Lawsons were always troubled by the frequent sound of heavy footsteps both inside and outside the house; sometimes the sounds were accompanied by the presence of an indistinct figure. Lawson, a distinguished classical scholar and a fellow of Pembroke College, claimed to see such a form on at least twenty-five occasions. Various members of the Lawson family also saw a ghost animal – about as frequently as the nun figure had been seen – probably thirty times, Lawson maintained, but never by two people at the same time.

A ghostly White Lady may have a similar provenance; possibly her presence in the garden near the entry to the abbey, within the present part-timber and part-brick house stems from some long-forgotten errand of mercy or act of charity, for often the quiet White Lady was seen in one of the bedrooms. A typical example of the reported appearance of this presence inside the house has been provided by the children of Dr Grey of Emmanuel College who complained, after the clergy had exorcised the whole house, that they were no longer tucked-up in their beds by 'the kind lady'.

Either or both of these ladies may have come to the house by means of an underground tunnel, from the old nunnery of St Radegund, now Jesus College, to meet with a monk. Some evidence for such a tunnel is provided by the presence of a bricked-up archway in the cellar of the present house. It is said that at one time such a clandestine meeting was discovered and the erring nun was walled-up alive – 'small wonder she haunts the place', Jimmy Wentworth Day said to me.

There are also reports of a phantom squirrel and a spectral hare here too. Both have been seen at the front of the house; the squirrel, a red one, now extinct in Cambridgeshire, runs along the grey wall and drops to the ground. It always disappears when the person who sees it approaches and thinks that there is no escape for the handsome and seemingly well-fed animal. The hare, a large one with floppy ears, is also seen in the garden, often when snow is on the ground, and it sits watching whoever sees it and then suddenly it is no longer there, and there are no traces of any animal in the snow. No one has ever suggested why these ghostly animals appear at certain places but perhaps they are some kind of atmospheric photograph that recurs under certain climatic conditions and disappears when conditions alter by the close presence of human beings; who can tell?

To complete the catalogue of ghostly manifestations at Old Abbey House there is, reportedly, a disembodied head and the eerie and totally unexplained sound of a clanking chain has been heard among other strange experiences. Some years ago now, when Professor Stratton was at Old Abbey House, he invited there many people who, like himself, took ghosts seriously: I remember there was a former colonel of the Royal Engineers, with the DSO and the Legion of Honour to his credit, a man who was also a deputy-lieutenant of the County of Cambridgeshire, director of the Solar Physics Observatory, former president of Caius College and a fellow of the Royal Society. If he took the hauntings that seriously, which he certainly did, as Jimmy Wentworth Day put it, 'you may be sure there was something in them'.

In 1968 a Mr Young lived with his daughter in the largest part of Old Abbey House and he told Jimmy Wentworth Day that when his daughter, a very level-headed young lady employed by the County Health Service, came to the house, some eight years earlier, 'the place was undoubtedly haunted'. She heard strange noises in the house and in the garden, night after night; sensed unseen presences repeatedly and, perhaps what is even more significant, her dog would suddenly take to rushing to one corner of a room or one part of the garden, its hair on end, and bark furiously – for no apparent reason. 'Dogs,' Jimmy used to say, 'I always regard as good witnesses.' Mr Young said that the previous tenant had been a lady and she also saw and felt some very frightening presences in the garden and occasionally inside the house. In the end she was glad to leave the place.

Earlier still, in the 1920s, the occupant had been a certain Mr Ascham and he welcomed Jimmy Wentworth Day and half-a-dozen undergraduate friends to the house, regaled them with stories of his many weird and frightening experiences and allowed them to sit up one night in the old house, all by themselves. It was his wife who had been terrified almost out of her wits by the sudden and ghastly appearance at chest-level of the apparition of a woman's head. Deathly white, without any body or arms or legs, it hovered in mid-air at the foot of her bed. Once, you might put down such an experience to a dream or hallucination, but Mrs Ascham saw the awful form on three occasions, always in the same room but in different positions; and even in mid-afternoon on one occasion as she entered the bedroom to fetch something. The form always hovered for a few moments, swaying slightly, backwards and forwards and from side to side, as though it found difficulty in remaining in one position and then, with a curious dip that always caught Mrs Ascham by surprise, the frightful appearance disappeared.

Before the Aschams moved into Old Abbey House, I was told, the two previous tenants both left the place in a great hurry, one of them at two o'clock in the morning. Neither ever returned to the haunted house with the haunted garden.

More recently poltergeist-like phenomena were reported, with various occupants and visitors complaining of indistinct forms and presences moving about the interior and exterior of the house at night, of sheets and bedclothes being suddenly twitched off the beds, and of groans and raps and rustling noises in the garden that had no rational explanation and the undoubted movement of very heavy furniture inside the house. After three local clergymen visited the house and exorcised the place with holy water and prayers, most of the uninvited and unwelcome guests seemed to depart but still, especially when the autumn afternoons draw in and the shadows lengthen around the long front of the house, an odd shadow or movement is noticed somewhere within or outside this lovable, warm old house, and the heart of the watcher skips a beat.

A recent visitor to Old Abbey House told me she encountered a mysterious lady in grey strolling around the garden; a figure she took to be a real person until it suddenly vanished and on making enquiries she was told no such person was resident or had visited the house. Perhaps with some justification Jimmy Wentworth Day always referred to the Old Abbey House, Cambridge, as 'the most haunted house in all England'. I often think of Jimmy Wentworth Day's words as we parted after talking long and hard about the case: 'You may be sure there is something very strange about Old Abbey House . . .'

OLD BATTERSEA HOUSE
Vicarage Road, Battersea, London

Surely one of the most historic, delightful and beautiful seventeenth-century properties extant, inside and outside, Old Battersea House is a gem of a place and haunted to boot. This ancient manor by the Thames has stood, outwardly little changed, dignified and serene, for more than two and a half centuries and it is still reminiscent of days long gone. It was built in 1699 by Sir Walter St John as a golden wedding present for his wife, Lady Joanna, and is said to be of Wren's design. The spacious oak staircase, just one of the features of this fascinating house, has seen most of the celebrated wits and notables during the passing years: the statesman, Lord Bolingbroke (1678-1751); Jean Voltaire (1696-1778) the French sceptic, dramatist and historian, while a fugitive during his sojourn in England; the poet, Alexander Pope (1688-1744); Lady Mary Rich, daughter of the 3rd Earl of Warwick; Joseph Addison (1672-1719), the essayist, poet and statesman; Sir Richard Steele (1672-1729), the essayist and dramatist; Jonathan Swift (1667-1745), the satirist; John Gay (1685-1732), the dramatist and poet; the great Duke of Marlborough; Charles Greville (1794-1865), the diarist; Lord John Russell (1792-1878), the 1st Earl Russell; Thomas Macaulay (1800 -1859), the historian and statesman; Francois Guizot (1787-1874), the French historian and statesman; the Prince Consort, Queen Victoria's beloved Albert visited the house twice, while other royal visitors have included Queen Mary and indeed there have been so many other distinguished celebrities and figures of note that it is small wonder that the staircase is itself haunted.

My friend Alasdair Alpin MacGregor has described one occasion when Lady Churchill was having tea one Sunday afternoon with her friend and owner of Old Battersea House, Mrs A. M. W. Stirling, when they were interrupted by the unexpected arrival of visitors desirous of being shown the house's art treasures, especially its collection of pre-Raphaelite paintings. While Mrs Stirling was thus engaged upstairs, Lady Churchill remained downstairs, in the hall, trusting her hostess wouldn't be absent too long. Mrs Stirling, on rejoining her shortly afterwards, noticed that she was curiously silent, seemingly strangely pre-occupied.

'There's something I particularly want to ask you about,' she eventually said. 'Will you and your husband come to tea on Tuesday, when we can discuss it?' Mrs Stirling duly accepted the invitation on behalf of herself and her husband; and on the appointed afternoon the Stirlings took tea with Lady Churchill.

'Tell me,' Lady Churchill began almost as soon as her guests were seated. 'Tell me. When I came to tea with you last Sunday, was there any friend with you in the house who might have been going to a fancy-dress ball?'

'At four o'clock on a Sunday afternoon?' answered Mrs Stirling. 'I should hardly have thought so!'

'Well, then, was there a pageant of any sort in the neighbourhood that afternoon? The kind of thing to which one would go in fancy dress?'

'Not as far as I am aware.' answered the increasingly puzzled Mrs Stirling.

'Let me tell you what happened,' Lady Churchill proceeded. 'While you were busy with the callers upstairs, as you know I waited alone downstairs, in the hall. I chanced to glance up and saw a man looking down over the banister. To my surprise he was carrying a sword and was wearing a plumed hat and a bright coat with remarkable diamond-shaped buttons. Through the balustrades of the landing I could see that he was also wearing jackboots. As I watched, puzzled and curious, he turned and came slowly downstairs towards me. I remember distinctly hearing the end of his sword striking against the oak stairs, as he descended, step by step. When he reached the bottom where I was standing, he took no notice of me, but rudely brushed past and made his exit through the doors to the garden room.'

'Did he remind you of anybody you had ever seen,' asked Mrs Stirling quietly.

'Well, if it weren't someone in fancy dress,' replied Lady Churchill. 'It was someone exactly like a painting I've seen of the Duke of Marlborough . . . yes, come to think of it I seem to remember the very odd arrangement of the eight buttons on his coat, two and two each side. But the Duke . . . well, did he ever visit Old Battersea House?'

'Tradition has it that he was a constant visitor,' Mrs Stirling explained. 'You see, he was a great friend of Bolingbroke.'

'So it was the Duke!' exclaimed Lady Churchill. 'And he shoved me aside because I'm a relative of his!'

I first met Mrs Stirling more than fifty years ago when I was visiting Alasdair Alpin MacGregor at his Swan Court, Chelsea flat where he was working on his latest book

131

when he chanced to mention his 'quite remarkable friend' Wilhelmena Stirling. She lived not far away at wonderful Old Battersea House, once the manor house of Battersea, and suddenly dropping the work he had in hand he said, 'Shall we go and see her?' And off we went.

When she learned that I was interested in ghosts Mrs Stirling said gaily: 'Spooks eh? Well, I am on the verge of becoming one myself so come in and we'll talk.' In fact she died in August 1965, a few days before her hundredth birthday but all thoughts of death or indeed any morbid thoughts were chased from my mind as I eyed the beauty that is Old Battersea House. I saw a house then that had seen better days but happily this fine treasure of domestic architecture, certainly the finest in Battersea, has now been wonderfully restored to its distinctive and impressive original character.

The house, formerly known as Terrace House and standing in seven acres of land, has had a chequered history. From the time it was built (a sundial on the south side is dated 1699) until the middle of the nineteenth century, some 150 years, it was the substantial home of various wealthy merchants and men of the professions and, as St John's College for Scoolmasters, it was also an educational training institution at one period.

Twice in the twentieth century the mellow old house has been in danger of demolition; in 1930 when it was acquired by Battersea Borough Council and in 1965 when the ownership reverted to Wandsworth Borough Council and it was found to be in a structurally unsound condition. Due entirely to the intervention of wealthy philanthropist Malcolm Forbes of the American Forbes Foundation, the house was taken on a ninety-nine-year lease on condition that the property was completely restored. You could look up from the basement and see the sky when Forbes first saw the fine old mansion. But after more than four years' renovation it was turned into a truly elegant and handsome residence – so much so that friends of the Forbes family used it whenever they could. When Ronald Reagan came to London to receive an honorary knighthood from the Queen he stayed there, sleeping in a four-poster bedstead, a bed that Elizabeth Taylor and other distinguished visitors had also occupied during visits to Old Battersea House.

In 1930, it was suggested that Sir Christopher Wren designed the house for the fiftieth wedding anniversary of Sir Walter St John but local historians say there is little evidence to support either of these claims and they say they have found no evidence that any of the St John family ever lived there. Others maintain that it was once the seat of Henry St John, Viscount Bolingbroke (1678-1751) who called it Bolingbroke House. It also seems to have been the occasional home of Alexander Pope (1688-1744) who wrote his *Essays on Man* in the Cedar Room, and Jonathan Swift is numbered among other visitors.

Although 1699 seems a likely date for the present structure, some of the brickwork used in the foundations is Tudor and it seems likely that a Tudor building once stood on the site, probably using the same ground plan and foundations. The first recorded resident is Peter DuBois, a City merchant of French Huguenot extraction, and the house is known to have then passed through the hands of the Otgers and the Defishers (both from Flanders) and the Longs, the Petts and the Devissors, all related to each other and all wealthy people of high standing connected with the City, the law, the Army, the Navy and local government.

The house then passed through other hands, including the original proprietors of the old Battersea Bridge, before a ten-year lease was acquired in 1828 by John George Shaw-Lefevre, a distinguished public servant and Clerk of the Parliament. Afterwards the house stood empty for a while and then Dr James P. Kay used the premises for training schoolmasters, a scheme he transferred to the National Society and as St John's College, it continued until 1923 when it was amalgamated with St Mark's College, Chelsea.

Then early in 1930 the whole site was acquired by the Battersea Borough Council who intended to demolish the building and replace it with council flats. After a public outcry, a preservation order was issued, and as various plans to use the house were being considered the council were approached by Mr and Mrs Stirling (the sister of Evelyn De Morgan) and they succeeded in obtaining a life tenancy on condition that their unique collection of pictures, pottery and porcelain by Evelyn and William De Morgan, contemporaries of William Morris, would be suitably displayed and open to the public by appointment at reasonable times.

By the time of Mrs Stirling's death, her husband having pre-deceased her, the house was in poor structural condition but provision had been made for the De Morgan Collection to be preserved and displayed at the house. However, Wandsworth Council, who now owned the house, found it impossible to meet the required funds and fortunately Mr Malcolm Forbes offered to restore the house at his own expense, if he could use part as private accommodation. And so it came about that Old Battersea House was restored and refurbished to its former glory.

On that first visit to Old Battersea House I well remember my attention being drawn to a fine carved fifteenth-century Italian armchair and I went to sit down in it but Mrs Stirling stopped me. She had been telling me about the strange and inexplicable raps she occasionally heard in the house, raps that seemed to have no possible rational explanation but which she said did seem to indicate some personal motive, yet they seemed gentle and kindly and she had almost come to regard them as affectionate. Then, 'No . . . no,' she said, firmly but not unkindly. 'Not that chair, dear; I keep that one for the ghosts.'

Among others who had asserted that the chair was haunted, I learned, was the late Lady Churchill. On one occasion Mrs Stirling, in Lady Churchill's presence, was about to seat herself in that particular chair when Lady Churchill seized her arm and prevented her from doing so. 'For heaven's sake don't sit there!' she exclaimed.

'Can't you see? There is a man already sitting there! He has a little, pointed beard and a big Elizabethan ruff. And he's got a rapier in his hand – and you were about to sit on his lap!'

Since that occasion Mrs Stirling tended to avoid occupying the 'haunted' chair and half-seriously dissuaded friends and visitors from doing so. On another occasion a visitor sat in the chair before she could prevent him doing so, but he jumped up immediately saying the chair felt icy cold and he had heard whispering close to his ear. For the rest of his visit to Old Battersea House he could hardly take his eyes off the chair but apparently nothing was visible to him. I remember Mrs Stirling telling me that she had no great objection to sitting on the lap of a ghost and may well have done so, unwittingly; but she had no desire to sit on a rapier, phantom or otherwise! Alisdair, on the other hand, who used to visit Old Battersea House a great deal at that time, told me he sometimes sat himself in the chair deliberately, 'though not necessarily incautiously', but he had never felt phantom occupant or phantom rapier – but he lived in hope! Sadly I fear, as far as that hope is concerned, he died in despair.

There is no doubt that some people have seen the unoccupied chair seemingly occupied. On one occasion Mrs Stirling was talking to a friend in the Garden Room while her little daughter was playing in the hall. Suddenly the child came into the room and said to her mother, somewhat shyly, 'Who is the man in the chair? He's wearing funny clothes and he won't talk to me . . .' By the time Mrs Stirling and her friend went to see for themselves, they saw only the empty chair and the little girl said, 'Man gone now'.

On yet another occasion Mrs Stirling told me that she was entertaining a friend in the beautiful Garden Room, where in fact we sat chatting, when suddenly her friend, who was facing the arched doorway leading to the hall and stairway, rose from her chair, smiling, as if to welcome someone and then, an astonished look coming over her face, resumed her seat. She said she had plainly seen an elderly lady about to enter the room but as she stood the figure completely vanished.

In 1988, after reading over my notes about Old Battersea House compiled some thirty years earlier, it occurred to me that it might prove to be an interesting event if I could organise a nocturnal visit to the historic house with some Ghost Club Society friends. I wrote to the resident administrator who told me she lived alone in the house for most of the time and had done so without any fear, although she was well aware that she had a ghostly resident. But she had come to accept this resident from the past and she felt the ghost accepted her presence and she would not want to stir things up by agreeing to our visit. I was able to reassure her on this point and she eventually agreed to our visit providing we avoided the times that Malcolm Forbes and his family and friends were in residence.

During the course of that visit I was accompanied by a dozen friends, including Dr Vernon and Elsie Harrison, Kenneth B. H. Lazenby, Philip Moore, Dennis Moyses and

Shirley Shaw and my wife. We spent a fascinating night in a truly fascinating house – not to mention the atmospheric garden.

Just a few days before our visit, we were told, a visitor had found something very distasteful about the hall (where once the haunted chair had stood) and she had the greatest difficulty in walking across the seemingly innocuous hall. Recently, we were also informed, there had been considerable interference with physical objects: pictures being removed from their hangings and propped against the wall; chairs moved from one side of a room to the other; a mirror moved and broken although no sound ever accompanied these disturbances. One day everything was as it should be and the next morning all sorts of things had happened without being touched by human hands.

The ghostly form of an elderly lady has been seen here, we were told, especially in the 'haunted' bedroom, and in the garden at the front of the house in the vicinity of the front door. A party who visited the house and felt the distinct presence of a phantom form afterwards claimed to have made contact with the presence, an elderly lady who was not happy with Americans being in possession of the house and making a lot of alterations – such as central heating and extra bathrooms – and it was felt that she could not settle in her old home.

This all sounded very much like the remarkable Wilhelmena Stirling whom I remember so well. I believe it is typical behaviour of the admirable Mrs Stirling who used to say 'Within and without this old house a changeless quietude prevails and its gracious rooms are haunted by the vanished past while what remains of the once glorious garden is often visited by the shades of those who walked and lingered there is days gone by.'

I think there is little doubt that the gentle shade of Wilhelmena Stirling has now joined the array of ghostly forms that haunt this delightful house and garden and I know we all agreed with one of my friends who said after our visit that he felt Old Battersea House was 'a little bit of heaven'.

During the night we spent there, with the spacious and elegant Garden Room as our Base Room, several members of our party felt that an elderly lady had come into the room from the front garden. Other reported incidents included the impression of a sweet scent on the top landing; a swishing sound outside the front doorway where there were several curious drops in temperature; snatches of music emanated through the house and garden from time to time, described to me by a musical friend present as 'probably Italian Renaissance music'; and one of the party glimpsed someone peering in through a window at the front of the house – it looked like an elderly lady and the witness thought at first it was one of the present party until she realised everyone was accounted for inside the house. When she looked again there was no sign of the 'person' she had seen, outside or inside the house.

A few days after our visit Ronald Reagan, a friend of Malcolm Forbes, stayed at Old Battersea House and was photographed in the haunted garden, sitting in the area where the ghostly old lady has most frequently been seen. I have often wondered whether he saw or sensed anything.

For me that night at Old Battersea House brought back happy memories and I am quite prepared to accept that Wilhelmena Stirling does return to the house and garden she knew and always loved, long, long ago. (But if it is her – who was the ghostly old lady seen in Wilhelmena Stirling's day?) And who can blame anyone for returning to such a place, so full of memories and encounters of days past? At Old Battersea House even when her ghost does not materialise, it is not difficult to believe that she is there, hovering in the wings as it were, and keeping an eye on things in that house of timeless charm that had once been her little bit of heaven.

THE OLD VICARAGE
Grantchester, Cambridge

It was Council Member of the Folklore Society and Oxford University lecturer, Christina Hole, who wrote a fascinating survey of English ghost-lore, who first told me about the haunted garden at the Old Vicarage, Grantchester, once the home of First World War poet, Rupert Brooke (1887-1915). Who can forget his haunting lines, 'If I should die, think only this of me:/ that there's some corner of a foreign field,/ That is forever England . . .' But he also wrote, of his haunted garden at Grantchester: 'Just now the lilac is in bloom,/ All before my little room;/ And in the flower beds, I think;/ Smile the carnations and the pink;/ And down the borders, well I know,/ The poppy and the pansy blow . . . would I were/ In Grantchester, in Grantchester!. . . the centuries blend and blur/ In Grantchester, in Grantchester.' This poem, entitled 'The Old Vicarage, Grantchester' was written in the Café des Westens, Berlin in May 1912 and ends with the much-quoted lines '. . . yet/ Stands the Church clock at ten to three?/ And is there honey still for tea?' Rupert Brooke did not die at Grantchester: he became ill on active service with the Royal Navy and died of sunstroke in Greece in 1915. At Grantchester today there is a pub named the Rupert Brooke with a sign depicting the young poet and the church clock with hands at ten to three.

Christina Hole told me that the long-time occupants, Dudley Ward and his wife, frequently heard unexplained footsteps coming up the garden towards the sitting-room and they became convinced that the footsteps were those of the enduringly popular young poet, whose reputation has been tarnished by revelations in a recent biography. Yet the fact that Brooke was greatly attached to the lovely house and garden can hardly be denied. At all events I lost no time in contacting and subsequently visiting the Wards and I too was enchanted by Brooke's Grantchester.

The garden then – this is some fifty years ago now – was largely unchanged since Rupert Brooke was there, and had influenced some of his most memorable poems and he wrote about 'the falling house that never falls'. I explored this odd little semi-ruined house at the bottom of the garden where, I was told, many curious poltergeist-like manifestations had taken place, especially at night when the place was totally deserted of any human being; small objects being spilled out of boxes and arranged in strange little patterns being a favourite lark. There were scores of instances when objects and furniture, both small and heavy, were moved with seemingly effortless ease about the place. On one occasion a large article of furniture was found in another room where it would have been very difficult if not impossible for it to be taken by normal means, the doorway being too narrow and the item in question having been in the room where it had always resided. The Wards told me they had taken the most stringent precautions to detect any normal explanation without any success.

Once, considerable disturbance had taken place among the articles in the quaint little house on a winter's night when it had been snowing all day but ceased in the early evening and was fine all night, yet, in spite of the undoubted movement of objects inside the building, there was no sign of footprints or disturbance of any kind in the snow around the strange little house which, I was told and completely accepted, could be a 'very eerie place after dark'. The Old Vicarage, Grantchester, is now occupied by author Jeffrey Archer. Lord Archer's wife, Mary, told me (2 December 1999) that she has never been sure which the original 'falling house that never falls' is; possibly Samuel Page Widnall's castle ruin which is now used as offices

137

and has an end fashioned as a deliberate ruin – or possibly the Old Vicarage itself which in Brooke's day was somewhat dilapidated.

The Wards told me they had heard footsteps, time without number, come up the garden, pass through the sitting-room that looked out towards the garden, mount the stairs and then walk about the top floor. At first they had been terrified but, in common with many people who experience manifestations in haunted houses, they had become accustomed to the disembodied footsteps and merely looked at each other and followed the direction of the footfalls with their eyes. On occasions the footsteps had also been heard by friends and visitors who happened to be present at the time. There did not appear to be any regular pattern with the sounds and they had been heard on weekdays and at weekends, in summer and in winter, in daylight and in darkness, although there did seem to be a preponderance for late afternoon and early evening. Once upstairs the sounds might continue for the best part of half an hour and sounded like someone walking about and moving books. The Wards wondered whether the ghost of Rupert Brooke was returning to his beloved Grantchester and once again sorting his books on the top floor as he must have often done during his lifetime.

In addition, ghostly forms have been glimpsed in the garden from time to time, forms that seem to be there one minute and gone the next, forms that do not seem to have any definite shape or individuality, forms that made no sound and forms that passed through trees and other obstructions without difficulty and forms that seem to come and go without rhyme or reason. But that such forms have been seen in the garden here is indisputable and may well have given rise to Brooke's poem containing the lines:

> And spectral dance, before the dawn,
> A hundred Vicars down the lawn;
> Curates, long dust, will come and go
> On lissom, clerical, printless toe;
> And oft between the boughs is seen
> The sly shade of a Rural Dean . . .

Always interested in ghosts and the paranormal in 1913 Brooke wrote some lines, suggested by some of the contents of the Proceedings of the Society for Psychical Research, which he called 'Sonnet'. It contained the lines

> Not with vain tears, when we're beyond the sun,
> We'll beat on the substantial doors, nor tread
> Those dusty high-roads of the aimless dead
> Plaintive for Earth; but rather turn and run
> Down some close-covered by-way of the air,
> Some low sweet alley between wind and wind,
> Stoop under faint gleams, thread the shadows, find
> Some whispering ghost-forgotten nook, and there
> Spend in pure converse our eternal day . . .

Just a few miles from Grantchester, to the west of Cambridge, stands Tudor Madingley Hall, with a terrace long haunted by the ghost of a pale-faced young man and the ghost of Lady Ursula Hynde that doubtless prompted Brooke to write:

> And things go on you'd ne'er believe
> At Madingley – on Christmas Eve.

Rupert Brooke counted among his friends John Drinkwater and Walter de la Mare, himself no stranger to ghosts. Both published books devoted to Brooke and his works. I recall on one occasion Walter de la Mare telling me of the time he almost saw a ghost. He was staying in a haunted house in Hertfordshire and 'in the grey hours just before daybreak' (as he put it) he found himself awake with the certain knowledge that there was a ghost in the room. He knew that he was fully conscious and awake, although he had not opened his eyes, and he lay there and reasoned with himself: if he turned his head and opened his eyes, he would see a ghost; then, whatever happened next, he would not get to sleep again for hours; better not to look. He kept his eyes closed and soon went back to sleep. Yet he told me he always regretted 'so abject a welcome' to one who probably meant him no harm and who would, in all probability, never visit him again. So Walter de la Mare created for himself a ghost: a ghost of memory and what might have been.

During a visit to The Old Vicarage at Grantchester the visionary Walter de la Mare, of Scottish and Huguenot ancestry and about whom there was a definite faerie atmosphere that was frequently evident in his exquisitely crafted poetry, told his close friend Rupert Brooke that he had seen spectral forms in the garden and his descriptions, admittedly vague and uncertain, nevertheless corresponded with forms that Rupert Brooke himself and visitors had claimed to see – at the same place, although neither Brooke nor de la Mare could find anything of a physical nature that might have misled the witnesses.

Dudley Ward and his wife had no shadow of a doubt about the place being haunted; they and many others heard unmistakable footfalls in the garden and in the house too, downstairs and upstairs, and they introduced me to three inhabitants of Grantchester who had not only heard the footsteps, presumably those of Rupert Brooke, but had also seen figures and forms in the garden. A former occupant, Elizabeth Clarke, used to insist that her garden was sometimes frequented by people unknown to her and at one time she suspected that the little house in the garden was being used by vagabonds for she distinctly saw figures of men in the vicinity but her dogs never barked (as they certainly would have done at an intruder) and she never found anything to suggest the place was being so used.

The ghostly form of George, Lord Byron, poet and ardent romantic, who was at nearby Trinity College from 1805 until 1808, has repeatedly been seen seemingly 'reliving' enjoyable times with friends in Grantchester which he often visited with other undergraduates to get away from the stern college officials, according to Rupert Matthews writing in 1993.

Although accepting that the house and garden today have 'great atmosphere' Dr Mary Archer tells me that nobody to her knowledge has 'experienced any strange or odd happenings since we have been here'. In 1993 Lord Archer denied all knowledge of any ghost and said he had never been bothered by anything like that.

Although Rupert Brooke may no longer typify the flower of British youth ruthlessly sacrificed in the 'war to end wars' his *Complete Poems*, published in 1932, show his affinity with such poets as Keats and his love for the Old Vicarage at Grantchester and its haunted garden cannot be denied.

PALACE OF VERSAILLES
Versailles, France

The wonderful Palace of Versailles was the principal residence of the kings of France from 1678 to 1769 and the beautiful gardens have been the scene of a number of ghostly happenings to different people on different occasions. None is more remarkable that the 'adventure' of two scholarly ladies of high integrity – a story that came to be regarded as one of the best authenticated ghost stories of all time and, whatever the explanation, is as strange and puzzling a story as anything to be found anywhere in the annals of psychical research.

Among the exquisite formal gardens, in the shady tree-lined pathways and amid such rural delights as a rustic bridge, a miniature ravine and a tiny waterfall – ghosts have walked.

Miss Annie Moberly, the daughter of a Bishop of Salisbury, was Principal of St Hugh's College, Oxford and her friend, Miss Eleanor Jourdain (seventeen years younger), the daughter of a Derbyshire vicar, was Vice-Principal elect of the same college. They visited Paris together in August 1901 and one day went to Versailles to look round the palace before visiting the Petit Trianon, which they had vaguely heard of as the little retreat that Louis XVI had presented to his Queen, Marie Antoinette, and where she and her court ladies reposed, rested and amused themselves. Little did they think they were about to walk into an experience which would change their lives.

They had some difficulty in locating the Petit Trianon and both ladies began to find the gardens depressing. The weather was pleasant enough, although the sky was overcast and a lively wind was blowing. Soon these academic colleagues in a strange place lost their way and began to feel lonely and mildly unhappy and at the same time they both noticed that the delightful cooling breeze had dropped and the landscape and trees suddenly appeared to be flat and almost two-dimensional, 'as though painted on canvas' as they put in their subsequent book. They walked on up a deserted drive, then 'crossed the drive' and reached a lake.

Miss Moberly noticed a woman shaking a white cloth out of the window of a building at the corner of a lane which they next entered, walking deeper and deeper into a mystery. A little further on they passed some more buildings and looked in at an open doorway, noticing the end of a carved staircase, but there did not appear to be anyone about and they did not like to go in.

They then discovered that there was a choice of three paths ahead of them and seeing two men some way ahead on the central path, they chose that way, caught up with the men and asked the way to the Petit Trianon and were directed straight ahead. They had noticed a wheelbarrow of some kind and a sort of pointed spade so the ladies at first assumed the men to be gardeners but they subsequently agreed that the figures

were wearing long coats and three-cornered hats and really seemed more like officials of some kind. Their enquiries seemed to be answered in a 'casual and mechanical way' but Miss Jourdain alone (it later transpired) saw, as they talked, a detached cottage with a woman and a girl standing in the doorway, dressed in clothes quite different to those of French people of 1901; they both wore white kerchiefs tucked into the bodice and the girl's dress (she appeared to be thirteen or fourteen) reached down to her ankles.

The two ladies walked on and reached a point where the path ended 'being crossed by another, right and left'. Ahead they saw a wood and inside the wood and overshadowed by trees, a circular garden kiosk with a man sitting close by. The man, who wore a cloak and a large hat, turned and looked at the visitors and something about his whole appearance filled them with such alarm that they decided to go

nowhere near him – but which way to go and who to ask? They were relieved to hear someone running towards them from the direction they had come, someone sounding out of breath and obviously in a great hurry; but when Miss Moberly turned round no one was in sight and then, almost at the same moment and with something of a shock, she perceived another man standing quite close to her and her friend. He was obviously a gentleman, tall and handsome with dark eyes and black curly hair under a large sombrero hat and he wore a dark cloak wrapped across him like a scarf. His face was red as though from much exertion and he seemed greatly excited and most anxious that they should proceed to the right. Miss Moberly had already decided to do just that and she and her friend set off towards a little bridge turning as she did so to thank the man for his assistance, only to find him no longer there – and again they heard the sound of running footsteps, seemingly close behind them.

Silently they passed over the rustic bridge which crossed a small ravine where a tiny waterfall cascaded down a green bank with ferns, so close they could have touched it. Beyond the bridge they followed a path through some trees, along the edge of a meadow bounded and overhung by more trees. Suddenly they came upon a house which they did not realise was there until they were close to it; a square, solidly built, small country house with tall, shuttered windows that looked north towards a garden in the English style, where in fact the ladies now found themselves. The north and east sides of the house boasted a terrace and on the grass, with her back to the terrace, a lady sat, sketching. She turned and looked full at the two visitors who noticed that she possessed a very pretty face although she was not particularly young and she wore a broad and shady white hat, a light summer dress that was long-waisted, cut low and rather old-fashioned looking. For some inexplicable reason Miss Moberly discovered that she felt annoyed at the presence of this lady; Miss Jourdain did not see her at all.

The two ladies stepped up on to the terrace of the house and at this point Miss Moberly had the odd feeling that she was acting out a dream. The oppressiveness and silence seemed unnatural. As the two friends crossed the terrace towards the south-west corner of the garden, they saw another house. A young man suddenly emerged from the doorway of this house, stepped out onto the terrace and banged the door behind him. He seemed to be some kind of footman, although he was not wearing livery, and he seemed to call to Miss Moberly and Miss Jourdain saying he would show them the way into the house. He gave the impression of being distinctly amused and led them to another entrance at the front of the house.

Once inside the building, which was in fact the Petit Trianon, a favourite residence of Marie Antoinette, our two ladies were kept waiting until the arrival of a French wedding party, a gay affair in which the visitors soon found themselves taking part, walking arm in arm to form a long procession round and through the rooms under the leadership of a guide. The two ladies felt quite revived again; they were interested in the wedding and in the contents of the Petit Trianon and they both felt happy and relaxed when they eventually took a carriage back to their hotel in Versailles, where they had some tea before walking to the station and back to Paris.

Oddly enough the ladies do not appear to have discussed or even mentioned their eventful afternoon trip to Versailles until a full week later when they discovered something very strange for while some of the people and surroundings had been seen by both of them, certain of the figures, objects and countryside had been seen by one of them and not by the other. Miss Jourdain learned that there was a tradition that on 5 October 1789 – the last time that Marie Antoinette went to the Trianon – she was sitting outside the front of the house in the English Garden, as she was in the habit of doing, when a page ran towards her bringing a letter from the palace warning the Queen of the approach of the mob from Paris. And Miss Jourdain was told that around the month of August the ghost of Marie Antoinette 'is regularly seen sitting in the front garden at the Petit Trianon, wearing a light flapping hat and a pink dress'. Both she and Miss Moberly discovered that it was in August (1792) that the Tuileries was sacked, the royal family escaping in the early morning. The ladies began to wonder whether during the hours of imprisonment before she went to the guillotine the Queen had gone back 'in such vivid memory to other Augusts she had spent at Trianon' that 'some impress had been implanted to the place'. The more they compared notes the more puzzled they became and finally they reached the conclusion that they must have 'stepped back in time' and had walked through the gardens of Versailles as they had been during the French Revolution on 1789, 112 years before their visit. The 'sketching lady', they decided, must have been Queen Marie Antoinette.

Subsequently both ladies revisited the gardens at Versailles independently and found the scenery greatly changed from their recollection of it and when they returned to the gardens together three years later they found virtually everything totally different: trees had vanished, as had the rustic bridge, the revine, the waterfall and the kiosk. They became more and more convinced that they had seen the place as it was in the reign of Louis XVI and Marie Antoinette. They became obsessed by their 'adventure' and spent the next ten years, on and off, researching the experience, the place, the history and the period after depositing records of their independent accounts at the Bodleian Library in Oxford (sadly these initial notes have never been located) and in 1911 Macmillan published their book entitled *An Adventure* which attracted considerable attention and went on to appear in some twenty impressions of five editions. The year that the book first appeared a member of the London Society for Psychical Research, M. Sage, explored the whole area and, as far as he could judge, retraced the ladies' footsteps and the sketch map he produced is still an excellent guide to the story.

It would appear that other people have experienced odd happenings at the haunted gardens of Versailles and although some of them insist they had never heard of the 'adventure' of Miss Moberly and Miss Jourdain it has to be said that it must be extremely unlikely that anyone visiting the gardens would not have heard of what quickly became a very famous ghost story, especially locally.

In 1914 an English family, Mr and Mrs Crooke and their son Stephen, told Miss Moberly and Miss Jourdain that in 1907 and 1908 they had lived at Versailles and all three of them together had twice seen the 'sketching lady', each time in the month of July but in the vicinity of the Grand Trianon. They never doubted that she was ghostly 'because of the peculiar way in which she appeared and disappeared'. Once too Mrs Crooke had encountered a man in eighteenth-century costume wearing a small three-cornered hat and both she and her husband had seen a woman in the gardens in an old-fashioned dress picking up sticks. Mr Crooke on one occasion had heard music coming over the water from the Belvedere where 'certainly none was being performed'. He said he had listened to the music for nearly a quarter of an hour.

In 1938 Mrs Elizabeth Hatton saw the figures of a man and a woman 'in fustian clothes' drawing a little wooden cart loaded with logs in the ornamental Versailles gardens. They passed close to Mrs Hatton but no sound accompanied the experience. As Mrs Hatton turned to see where the figures went, she discovered they had vanished. In 1949 Jack and Clara Wilkinson and their young son saw a woman in a gold-coloured crinoline-type dress outside the Grand Trianon; a moment later the figure had disappeared.

In 1912 there was published a report of a visit by Robert and Margaret Gregory to the Petit Trianon 'about a year before *An Adventure* was published' stating that one of them saw a woman leaning out of a window shaking a 'table-cloth' and also a couple of gardeners or labourers. Struck by the experience of Miss Moberly and Miss Jourdain they had returned to the gardens at Versailles and to their surprise neither of them recognised a single thing! They found no trace of the trees and houses they had both seen and instead of the thick wood they had walked through there was now a broad open path.

Miss Clare Burrow and Miss Annie Lambert explored the great palace at Versailles in 1928 and saw figures in out-of-date costumes and heard voices that frightened them in the gardens around the Petit Trianon.

In 1955 a London solicitor and his wife visited the gardens and after experiencing an 'extraordinary feeling of tenseness in the air' they saw three clear figures in brilliant eighteenth-century costume who suddenly disappeared.

When I was researching my volume *Hauntings – New Light on the Greatest True Ghost Stories* (Dent, 1977) I was in touch with Dr Joan Evans, the distinguished historian, archaeologist and copyright owner of *An Adventure* and she told me she had become convinced that the ladies had walked into a rehearsal for a *tableau vivant* by Comte Robert de Montesquiou-Fezensac and his friends who were in the habit of staging such events in the gardens of Versailles in eighteenth-century costume and she had decided not to permit any further publication of Miss Moberly and Miss Jourdain's book. Dr Evans told me: 'The bona fides of the ladies are impeccable but they did make a great fuss about very little'. I am not sure that the Versailles mystery is that easily explained.

I recall discussing this fascinating case with Dr C. E. M. Joad, the famous philosopher – who followed in the footsteps of Miss Moberly and Miss Jourdain in the company of Harry Price in 1934 – and my contemporaneous notes reveal exactly what he said: 'These two women met and addressed persons wearing the costumes of 1789, some of whom were visible to one lady, others to both. They saw woods which are no longer there; passed by a rustic bridge over a revine down which ran a cascade, which no longer exists; they saw a man sitting by a garden kiosk, which is not to be found; and were accosted by a footman who emerged from a door in the palace which, through the destruction of a staircase, has ceased for nearly a hundred years to afford any exit'. He went on to ask, what possible explanation are we to give? He thought there were three main possibilities and he himself favoured the third. The first is the theory of reincarnation which, he felt, falls from lack of evidence. The second possibility is that we see ghosts but the fact that the ladies also saw trees, bridges, ravines and scenery in general he found incredible. The third possibility, which he believed was increasingly forced upon us on other grounds –that there is something very odd about time. We cannot see what does not exist, the future and the present must be 'there', so to speak, in order that we can see into them. 'The more we think about time the more puzzling it becomes,' he said. (I remember J. B. Priestley saying something very similar) 'A future which is "there" already fixed and existing, seems to deprive us of free will and a past that is "there" means that there is a very real sense in which we have not yet begun to live. In fact, in the present state of our knowledge, the problem is beyond us.'

The worst storm in the history of the Palace of Versailles took place on Boxing Day 1999 when trees planted by Napoleon and Marie Antoinette were among the victims. Experts described the gardens the day after as a 'scene of complete devastation'. Many trees were completely uprooted; all the principal avenues were wrecked. The Trianon garden was strewn with broken branches; some 10,000 trees were down including important trees planted by Louis XVI in 1774. Gardeners literally wept at the awful sight – but will it affect the ghosts in what had been one of the most beautiful of all haunted gardens? Visiting in 2008, I found it restored and perfect – but I saw no ghosts.

RAFFLES HOTEL
Beach Road, Singapore

Raffles is arguably the most famous hotel in the world, certainly the most nostalgically named of any hostelry anywhere and it has always been known affectionately in practically every corner of the world quite simply as 'Raffles'. And it has a haunted garden.

In the enthusiastic atmosphere of Queen Victoria's Golden Jubilee, when Singapore was one of the busiest ports in the world, the American Sarkies brothers, Martin and Tigram, hotel entrepreneurs, were seeking to expand and looking for the right location for an elegant and luxurious hotel. Sitting in Captain George Dare's garden on Beach Road, they looked at the sea-frontage with plenty of space for shady gardens, well removed from the hubbub of the harbour yet close to the huge, grassy Padang and they both knew instinctively that they had found the right place. The nearby Raffles Institution had been founded by Sir Stamford Raffles (1781-1826), the founder of Singapore, and within hailing distance there was the new statue of Sir Stamford that had been created in the middle of the Padang, but the house the Sarkies brothers were now interested in was occupied by the Raffles Girls' School; however, they found they were able to lease the property in the summer of 1886 and they lost no time in setting about restoring and enlarging the old mansion, although they had yet to decide on a name for the hotel. They were aware that their hotel would be replacing the Raffles Tiffin Room and the Raffles Girls' School and that it was facing the Raffles Institution; the obvious became a stroke of genius when they decided to call the new hotel Raffles.

The original Raffles Hotel opened its doors for the first time on 1 December 1887 and the passing years have seen enormous alterations and changes before we arrive at the sumptuous and unique establishment that is Raffles today; and within a very short time of the opening famous people from all walks of life were visiting and have continued to visit ever since. And Raffles possesses one of the really great bars in the world: The Long

Bar where, in 1915, the head barman Ngiam Tong Boor invented two of the world's most famous cocktails, the Million Dollar and the Singapore Sling. Today the marble floors, the enormous fans, the doormen resplendent in white and the swimming pool on the roof surrounded by bougainvilleas is a perfect paradise, but even in the early days Raffles was a magnet for the famous and the discerning.

One of the first guests could well have been Joseph Conrad (1857-1924); he has written about the hotel but does not name it – explicitness, he used to insist, is fatal to all artistic work(!) – but he describes the luxury and a view over the sea and there is little doubt that he is talking about Raffles; certainly the management have no doubts and today there is a suite in the hotel named after him. In Raymond Flower's *Meet You at Raffles* (Times Books, Singapore, 1988), which has been a great help to me in compiling this account, we are told Conrad 'very likely' spent a lot of the time in the garden where he could well have become acquainted with the reputed ghosts which he subsequently used in some of his vivid short stories: he was a writer whom Boris Karloff admired all his life and in his collection *Tales of Terror* (World Publications, New York, 1943) Karloff includes a story by Conrad who, he points out, 'had the power of creating suspense and terror through suggestion,' not realising in all probability, that Conrad knew the real fear that comes with encountering the supernatural.

Soon Conrad was followed by Rudyard Kipling who, in turn, may well have found the genesis of some of his grisly and powerful stories, 'fine and deeply moving efforts of the imagination' Somerset Maugham called them, in the haunted gardens of Raffles Hotel. In the years that followed, right up to the present day, prominent personalities, of all persuasions, visited Raffles and many experienced the delights and the mysteries of the gardens.

An early visitor was the Duke of Sutherland accompanied by Mrs Caddy speedily followed by other dukes, crown princes, maharajahs and people like Herman Hesse, Somerset Maugham, Noel Coward, John Mills, Frank Buck (of 'Bring 'em Back Alive' fame), Charles Chaplin, Maurice Chevalier, Ronald Coleman, Norma Shearer, Jeanette MacDonald, Jean Harlow, Dr Serge Voronoff (who pioneered the monkey gland treatment), Robert Kennedy, Ava Gardner, Leslie Charteris (the 'Saint' author whose real name was Leslie Charles Bowyer Yin and he was born in Singapore), Douglas Fairbanks and his son Doug Fairbanks Jnr, Mike Todd, Paulette Goddard, Mary Pickford, Elizabeth Taylor, Tyrone Power and Linda Christian, Orson Welles, Alfred Hitchcock, Richard Burton, Marlon Brando, Lord Mountbatten of Burma, Emperor Haile Selassie, James Callaghan, Harold Wilson, Anthony Eden, Ingrid Bergman, Grace Kelly, Hayley Mills and Trevor Howard (working on 'Pretty Polly' filmed in the hotel) and still name-dropping, other visitors have included Margaret Thatcher, the present Duke of Kent, Dr Robert Runcie, Archbishop of Canterbury and Rolf Harris.

Raffles itself (one of nine buildings in Singapore preserved as an historic monument) and its gardens have long been reputed to be haunted. Raymond Flower, in his work already cited, refers to guests repeatedly hearing the voice of a little girl singing 'Mary Had a Little Lamb' coming from the garden. One manager used to scold staff for leaving burning joss-sticks in the corridor for the purpose of evicting the restless spirits in the garden.

A number of visitors claim to have encountered the ghost of Somerset Maugham in the vicinity of Raffles. He certainly enjoyed his visits and no doubt, if he could, he would return but it is more likely, if his form has been seen, that a pictorial echo from the past has become imprinted on the atmosphere and, at certain times and under certain conditions, reappears.

A few years ago a person interviewed on BBC Radio 4 told of hearing the disembodied voice of a schoolgirl singing an English nursery rhyme; something that has been reported, it transpires, since before 1886 when Raffles Girls' Boarding School occupied the site.

In the autumn of 1990 a long-standing and respected Ghost Club Society member, Jennie E. Newlands, told me she had visited Singapore and, staying at Raffles Hotel, she had been awakened in the middle of the night on the day of her arrival by the sound of a girl's voice, from the direction of the deserted garden below her window. Being interested in such matters she made enquiries at every opportunity during her stay and located nearly a dozen instances of similar unexplained sounds and disturbances during the previous few years; sometimes figures of schoolgirls had been glimpsed in the garden, figures that seem to melt into the background once they were observed and under observation. I was told the staff at Raffles have known all about these happenings for years.

ROSE HALL GREAT HOUSE
Montego Bay, Jamaica

Two members of The Ghost Club Society spent a memorable holiday at Rose Hall Great House, Jamaica, and afterwards they presented me with relevant books and photographs, told me the colourful story of the legendary haunting and acquainted me with stories of the ghosts that have long haunted the house and garden of that famous Jamaican landmark.

Two hundred years ago Rose Hall was one of the grandest mansions in the land but then, for many years, it stood abandoned, crumbling – and haunted. Once its magnificent folding doors hand-carved in solid mahogany, its circular staircase of sandalwood and its opulent gilded furniture was the talk of the whole Caribbean for it was the home of the richest of the sugar lords of Jamaica towards the end of the eighteenth century.

The story of Rose Hall Great House really begins in 1746 when one Henry Fanning purchased a plantation called 'True Friendship', some 290 acres of rolling sugarcane land, bounded by the sea. He married a lovely woman, Rosa Kelly, but Fanning died six months after the wedding and in 1750 the widowed Rosa married a planter named George Ash, to whom the building of Rose Hall Great House has been attributed but

the house he built for his bride was in fact a forerunner to the historic and infamous Rose Hall. Ash died in 1752 leaving Rosa a widow once more – but a wealthy one. She married her third husband in 1753. He was the Hon Norwood Witter, an avaricious man who liberally helped himself to the available wealth at Rose Hall for thirteen years until he died in 1766. The lovely Rosa still had suitors and she married for a fourth time in 1767. The Hon John Palmer, a widower with two sons in England, became master of Rose Hall, along with the neighbouring estate of Palmyra which he owned, and it was he who built Rose Hall Great House between 1770 and 1780, indisputably the finest residence in Jamaica and for over twenty happy years John and Rosa Palmer enjoyed the magnificent house in its brilliant setting and then Rosa died, in 1790, leaving all her property to her husband John.

John Palmer married his third wife in 1792, a girl of twenty named Rebecca Ann James. He died just five years later leaving Rose Hall and Palmyra in trust for his two sons, John and James, their survivors and heirs and failing such heirs to the sons of his nephew James Palmer. The young widow, Rebecca Ann Palmer, left Jamaica for England soon after her husband's death. John and James Palmer, the sons of the first marriage, were absentee landlords and both died in England without ever having visited Jamaica. Neither had children. Rose Hall and Palmyra thus reverted to the Hon John Palmer's grand-nephew, John Rose Palmer. He quickly set about taking possession and looking after his properties which had been badly handled for some twenty years. In 1820 John Palmer married Annee May Patterson – the beautiful Annee Palmer who will always be regarded as the evil occupant of Rose Hall.

According to Rex Nettlefold, Departmental Head at the University of the West Indies in Kingston and prominent Jamaican author, Annee Palmer had a lovely complexion, a rich voice, black penetrating eyes, smooth black hair and a small nose and mouth. She could be gentle, smiling – even childlike, some said, but she was also haughty, cruel, impatient and easily provoked. She was to marry three times and take numerous lovers, many of whom would meet untimely deaths when they no longer pleased her.

Annee seems to have been about eighteen or so when John Palmer married her and he had no idea of what lay beneath her desire to please, her apparent innocence and her insistence that the talk of wickedness in her past was idle gossip. In fact Annee's background was shrouded in mystery and sorcery. Her mother was English, her father an Irish merchant who went to Haiti attracted by the opportunity of making money under King Christophe who encouraged white people to settle there. Even as a little girl Annee had become interested in voodoo and soon she became the favourite of a high voodoo priestess who in turn held considerable influence in King Christophe's court. Widowed and childless, she took to Annee and was always showering her with gifts, at first trinkets but soon quite valuable items. Annee's parents, thinking the influence the priestess had with the king could well benefit them, encouraged the friendship. Soon Annee was learning about spirits, good and bad, and about the air being charged with the supernatural over which she could exert control. Before long she was attending secret voodoo orgies and learning power of suggestion in drumbeats in the dead of night. She soon realised and envied the fear people had of the high priestess and she eagerly absorbed all she could of voodoo and black magic and the powerful effect these could have on people. Within a few years Annee was convinced by the persuasive powers of the priestess that she almost had the powers of a god herself, but just as she was beginning to feel the reflected power and glory of her friend and benefactor, the priestess died, soon followed by both of Annee's parents. A white girl isolated among slaves who already believed she had the power and ability to cause death and destruction, who believed she spied on them and could conjure up fiery apparitions that could spell doom for all who saw them, Annee realised that Haiti was a bad place for her. She considered going to England but she dreaded the conformity that would have entailed and instead she went to Tahiti and then to Jamaica where she met and married John Palmer, then aged 72.

After seven years of marriage John Palmer died; he was no match for her wily schemes and Annee claimed he drank himself to death. At all events she soon took another wealthy man to Rose Hall as her husband but he went mad (or so it was said); and there was a third who could well have married her for her money; he allegedly died of apoplexy – anyway he too was soon dead. All natural causes, claimed Annee, but the slaves told tales of agonised groans, of piercing screams, of muffled bangs and crashing sounds and they whispered of poison, stabbing and strangulation . . .

Irremovable blood stains on the beautiful floor of one room remained as silent witness to violence and when the stories began to become common knowledge Annee had the room closed and sealed, although there were still tales of strange and frightening noises emanating from the empty room and parts of the enormous garden.

After the death of her third husband Annee ran the plantation alone for eleven years, with the help of an overseer and a few other supervisors, usually white men who were outcasts, rogues and scoundrels from English society who cared little about the slaves or how they were treated and Annee put up with their drinking, their cruelty, and their cohabiting with the slaves as long as she could rely on them to get the plantation work done and keep the profits rolling in. Sometimes Annee even allowed them to become her lovers but she never lost her contempt for them and she mercilessly got rid of them when the fancy took her. What did change was the atmosphere of happiness that had long pervaded the great house, its gardens and the plantation. Instead there were frequent stories of scandal, of cruelty, brutality and harshness and tales of trouble, misadventure, barbarity and unexpected and unexplained deaths. The majestic mansion came to be shunned and feared, a place where the slaves, once so happy, bowed in terror before their mistress as she strode

among them, frequently choosing a well-built young negro for her 'personal servant', a slave upon whom she lavished every comfort until she was tired of him when he would often conveniently disappear.

Soon her stepson caught her eye, he was young and good-looking and quickly yielded to her advances; yet her hold over the young Palmer was not complete and unbeknown to her she shared his affections with a beautiful young mulatto slave girl. One of Annee's charge-hands, humiliated when he lost his position of favour, sought revenge and told his mistress of the young Palmer's interest in the mulatto girl. In those days there was no law to prevent an owner from killing a slave if he so wished and the young girl was flogged and painfully put to death, watched by the scornful Annee who insisted that her stepson watched too. But this vicious act of cruelty had the opposite effect to what Annee Palmer hoped and the young Palmer, sick with horror, left the island and never returned. Gradually Annee Palmer and Rose Hall Great House came to be shunned and avoided by those who had once been her husband's friends and the sounds of screams and anguished cries filled the night air around Rose Hall as she took her revenge on the slaves with whips and sadistic torture.

Despite her many lovers and the floggings that so excited her Annee was always restless for new exhilaration and one of these distractions was to change into male

155

attire and ride round the property of an evening, laying to with her whip on the backs and bodies of any of the slaves she came across. She never forgot the voodoo and obeah she had been taught as a girl and there are records to show that she had the power to go into a trance-like state and project harm to selected victims who swore they saw apparitions that led them to perform acts of wickedness over which they had no control or sometimes do harm to themselves. Doctors said they could do nothing for a slave who was convinced that he was under such a spell, sometimes a death spell, and unless an obeah chief was successful in exorcising or overcoming the evil spirit, the victim died. It was rumoured that a frightening apparition had been seen by everyone at Rose Hall plantation on the night of John Palmer's death.

Then one day the evil cloud that had hung for so long over Rose Hall lifted for one day in 1831 Annee Palmer was murdered in her bed by the half-crazed slaves who she had tortured almost daily. Her body did not ever receive burial but long after her death her bones were thrown disdainfully under a tree in the east garden where the grave, such as it was, can still be seen, long overgrown and surrounded by other trees. Perhaps that is why her ghost has never rested for the wicked Annee Palmer has long been said to haunt Rose Hall Great House, inside and outside, and even when the place was deserted, screams and cries of terror were frequently heard, echoing from the empty rooms and tales of tragedy continued long after she was gone. The last caretaker when the house was empty fell down the stone steps leading to the cellar and broke his neck – local people say he was pushed by the ghost of Annee Palmer and there were other strange calamities reported by visitors as the great house slowly but surely fell into decay. But still the ghost walked. Responsible Ghost Club Society members have reported encountering odd and unexpected figures and experiencing peculiar happenings and activity in the shell of the house and in the overgrown and abandoned garden. One figure, that of a commanding and strident woman flitting noiselessly about the place, was reportedly seen time and time again – even after the great house had been restored.

In 1971 there was an inaugural tour of the newly-restored Rose Hall Great House attended by the head of the elected government of Jamaica and guests from every walk of life and from all parts of the world admired the beauty that is Rose Hall. Today this truly splendid property is one of the most popular tourist attractions in Jamaica and the Caribbean and you can enjoy food and drink amid the arches, heavy beams and stone caverns of the lower dungeon and you may be able to visit Annee Palmer's bedroom – the source of many unknown and untold tales – and perhaps you may even encounter, either here or in the atmospheric garden, the ghost of 'the white witch of Rose Hall' herself, the subject of an undying legend: a woman who met a deserved if untimely end and the house and garden that she knew still harbours the essence of times past.

ROYAL BOTANICAL GARDEN
Madrid, Spain

In 1990 I was invited to take part in a four-hour long live television programme in Madrid with other contributors from Spain, Germany and Italy. Once we were established in the luxurious Westin Palace Hotel in the centre of the city facing the Neptuno fountain and the Prado Museum, my wife and I came downstairs and there across the foyer were our old friends, Eric and Dora Maple!

The Palace Hotel has been a magnet for artists, writers and bohemians in general since it opened its doors in 1912. Pablo Picasso and Luis Bunuel loved to hang out in La Rotonda, the spectacular circular lounge crowned by an enormous stained glass dome, Salvador Dali was often to be seen strolling around the lobby trailing an ocelot on a gold chain and Ernest Hemingway practically lived in the bar, drinking dry martinis with the famous bullfighters of the day.

Eric Maple was a knowledgeable and erudite expert on witchcraft and he too had been invited to take part in the mammoth live TV programme – two Ghost Club Society members meeting halfway round the world to join in a global exploration of the paranormal! It was certainly a fascinating experience with the various contributions and interviews being translated into the various languages of all those taking part, simultaneously – but that is another story!

The guests on the programme were given the opportunity of visiting various parts of the city and we also visited Toledo but Eric and Dora visited the beautiful public gardens almost opposite the Palace Hotel and seemingly encountered a ghost of which they had no previous knowledge.

Idly walking through the deserted but exceedingly pleasant and peaceful gardens, Eric and Dora became aware of someone following them, as they meandered through the Rosaeda, they thought it was. The impression, and they both said it was really no more than that for they could not recall actually hearing any footsteps, continued until they saw a seat ahead and they decided to deposit themselves there and see who it was that seemed to be following them.

Hurrying a little they reached the seat and sat down, looking as they did so in the direction they had come and they saw a girl who seemed to be no more than eighteen or nineteen, they thought. She was dressed in a light and colourful dress which Dora thought rather odd since it was February, but the weather was mild and she thought perhaps the girl lived nearby. As they watched, the girl hurried on her way, not looking in their direction or seeming to be aware of their presence. As she proceeded along the straight and deserted path ahead, Dora and Eric rose from the seat and followed. For the life of them they could not think why they did that but something seemed to tell them this was no ordinary girl, although she looked absolutely normal in every way. After walking for perhaps five minutes, without seeing another single person,

Dora and Eric decided this was all rather pointless and they decided to take the next path in whatever direction it led and make their way back to the hotel.

As they made this decision, which they quietly agreed between them, Eric looked beyond the girl ahead to see whether there was a path they might take; then suddenly he realised the girl had vanished! There was nowhere she could have gone, the path was straight, the flowerbeds bordering the path were low and there were no bushes or shrubs or buildings or anything that could have explained her sudden disappearance. Almost unable to believe their eyes, Dora and Eric hurried forward, then looked back, looked everywhere in fact but there was no doubt about it: the girl had simply vanished and there was no rational way she could have done so.

Back at the hotel Dora and Eric related what had happened and then learned for the first time that the figure of a young girl, wearing a summer dress, has been reported for years, always walking along one particular path (the one Dora and Eric had traversed) before suddenly and inexplicably vanishing. No one seemed to know who she was or why she appeared although there was a vague story concerning a young visitor who had been walking in the gardens one summer day with her fiancé when he had a sudden and completely unexpected attack of paralysis and in falling struck his head on a projecting stone and died instantly. It is thought by some people that the girl revisits the scene of the traumatic event and certainly she has been seen by scores of people over the years who are themselves visiting that haunted garden.

When they spoke of their experience back at the Palace Hotel the Maples were overheard by a member of the staff who volunteered the information that it was not the best-known and most frequently seen ghost in the Gardens that they had seen. This was the unidentified ghost of a running man who had been reportedly seen times without number in various parts of the Gardens. He is dressed in early eighteenth-century costume with high shirt collar, elaborate shirt front, stout jacket with velvet collar and fancy waistcoat – much as the portrait of Goya by Vicente López (1772-1850) in the nearby Prado Gallery.

I am indebted to Juan Armada, the Curator of the Real Jardin Botanico, for his kind assistance in the preparation of this entry.

St James Hotel
Cimarron, New Mexico, USA

This historic hotel, once a gambling hall and saloon, has long had the reputation of being haunted in various rooms but in 1994 I heard about the apparent haunting of the exterior or garden.

St James Hotel was opened in 1880 and the place soon saw plenty of action. Cimarron, Spanish for 'wild' and 'unbroken', was a favoured stop on the famous

Santa Fe Trail, that made possible extensive commerce with the rest of the United States, first with pack animals and from 1822 by wagon trains from Independence and Kansas City; Santa Fe being the capital of New Mexico and the oldest seat of government in the United States. A stone in the plaza marks the end of the old Santa Fe Trail. So Cimarron and especially the saloon, built by Frenchman, Henri Lambert, personal chef to President Abraham Lincoln and to General Ulysses S. Grant, became a regular stop for traders, mountain men and desperados. Violence was by no means unknown within these thick adobe walls and indeed there is evidence to support the local claim that at least twenty-six people met violent death here, as the bullet holes in the tin ceiling bear witness.

The notorious gunman Clay Allison is said to have danced on the bar, once part of the present elegant dining room, and other notables who stayed at the St James in days gone by include train robber Blackjack Ketchum and Buffalo Bill Cody who met here with Annie Oakley to plan his Wild West Show. Novelists, including Zane Grey (1875-1939), famous for his Westerns including *Riders of the Purple Sage* (1912) – which sold over a million copies and made its author's fortune – and Governor of New Mexico, Lew Wallace (1827-1905), author of *Ben Hur* (1880), wrote some of their works at the St James Hotel, while artists, including Frederic Remington (1861-1909), the illustrator, painter and sculptor who specialised in North American Indians as seen on their eastern plains, sketched and painted the nearby hills in this land of enchantment. There is also a room named after Bat Masterson, the famous Dodge City lawman and gunfighter who stayed at the St James in 1887.

Today the hotel with its fifteen rooms restored and beautifully decorated and furnished describes itself as a place of quiet elegance, good food and drink, expert and friendly service and unsurpassed hospitality. And there is much to commend the St James in this magnificent and interesting part of the old American West and not least the ghosts. Room 18 has long been reputed to be haunted by an unpleasant ghost who

manifests as something like a 'swirling energy field'. When a former owner, Pat Loree, was showing Dr Kenneth Wright the room one night in 1986 they encountered 'something' that she described as a 'not-so -friendly ghost' coming at them out of the room. 'It came down on me and passed on my right and I felt like I was struck at,' she said in 1991. 'I fell to my knees and got back up and at that point it came back at me and knocked me back on my knees and then went to the corner of the room where it seemed to spin and swirl . . .' Thereafter Room 18 was closed to the public. A later owner said: 'We have never had anyone sleep in there – not with the things that are always going on . . .'

Friendlier 'spirits', if that is what they are, seem to delight in tormenting new employees in the Kitchen and Dining Room areas, bursting glasses, relighting candles and repeatedly moving objects. Sometimes 'a small man with a pockmarked face' has been glimpsed inside and just outside the hotel and he is blamed for the mischievous happenings and has been dubbed the 'Little Imp'. A more gentle presence, thought to be the ghost of the original owner's wife who died in the affected room while still young, heralds her appearance by a waft of fragrant perfume: the room is predictably known as Mary's Room. A quiet, gentle shade from the past, revisiting the scenes of her all too brief happiness, this ghost too has been seen in the garden area of this atmospheric hotel.

An American correspondent tells me that he and his wife thought they would visit St James Hotel in 1998, having heard about the allegedly haunted rooms. They were surprised, on their arrival, late one wet evening, to see a young lady apparently sheltering near the front entrance. As they approached, thinking perhaps she could not open the door, she suddenly disappeared! It was quite impossible for her to have disappeared from their view in any normal way; the door was still firmly closed and walls on each side of the door prevented her from going either to the left or to the right of the front door. Later they learned that they had probably encountered the ghost of Mary who usually confined herself to Mary's Room but other people had occasionally reported seeing a young woman outside the hotel who disappeared suddenly and inexplicably.

St James Hotel, Cimarron, justly labels itself the hotel 'where history was made'; they might almost have added, 'and where historic personages reappear . . .'

SUTTON PLACE
Guildford, Surrey

This spacious Tudor mansion near Guildford was once owned by publishing and real estate tycoon, art collector and companion of actress Marion Davis for thirty-two years, William Randolph Hearst who built and lived in the legendary, extravagant and unique San Simeon castle in California, but when I first knew this corner of England it was owned and occupied by another American millionaire, Jean Paul Getty, and he and I talked about ghosts and the haunted garden at Sutton Place.

The ancient manor house was built in the years 1523 to 1525 by Sir Richard Weston, a favourite of King Henry VIII. It is one of the earliest extant specimens in England of a mansion house built wholly as a peaceful dwelling entirely without any thought of defence. Up to this time all houses in the country of any importance or size were built either as actual castles or castellated mansions or at the very least in the form and in the spirit of a castle; now it was decided that the wars of the barons were over and a gentleman might live at his ease under the protection of law and the King's peace. Is this why quiet ghosts have walked at Sutton Place for centuries?

Sir Richard Weston and his wife enjoyed their new home, Sudtone as it is described in Domesday, and after their only son, who had been a playmate of the King, was accused of being one of the lovers of Anne Boleyn and was beheaded on Tower Green, his young widow (a rich heiress in her own right) lived at Sutton Place. Two years after her ascension Queen Elizabeth I visited Sutton Place and sojourned there for three days.

Today the house is much as it was when first built with many of its treasures there for all to see. Without detailing each room perhaps it will suffice to say that the Great Hall is over fifty-five feet in length and more than twenty-five feet wide and nearly thirty-one feet in height. The fourteen windows – having ninety-two separate panes of glass – are all decorated with shields and quarries of painted glass, one coat or set of devices in each pane, hardly one without some relationship to the founder or his family.

Sir Richard Weston was a remarkable man and evidently a person who could bend with the wind of change. He served the King for thirty-three years through Henry's passions in rule, in religion, in friendship, in love and retained the confidences successively of William Warham, legal expert and royal confident; Sir Thomas More, lawyer, statesman and saint; Sir Thomas Wolsey, cleric, statesman and chaplain to the King; Thomas Cromwell, the Earl of Essex and the 1st Earl of Bedford. The wily old knight served with the Bouchiers, the Fitzalans, the Howards, the Stanleys, Berkeleys and Brays, whose arms and coronets and garters are proudly displayed in the Hall while there and elsewhere in this house can be found the devices of Aragon and Castille, the pomegranate of Catherine, Jane Seymour's phoenix arising from the flames, the arms and portrait of Queen Mary side by side with the devices of Queen Elizabeth I and the portrait and escutcheons of her cousin and hostess.

In addition to pictures of Henry VIII (after Holbein), Queen Elizabeth I (after Zuccaro) and paintings by Romney, Tintoretto, Landseer, Reynolds and Durer there are priceless Brussels tapestries, seventeenth-century embroidery and painted glass of extraordinary beauty and rarity. In truth the ghosts at Sutton Place walk on hallowed ground.

The most common ghostly visitor to Sutton Place seems to be a mysterious Lady in White who has been seen with some frequency in the garden or rather in the grounds, some 775 acres in fact. Dorothea St Hill Bourne was one witness who told me she saw the unidentified figure quite distinctly when accompanying J. Paul Getty on a stroll along the Yew Path. They both saw the noiseless form at the same time and Getty told Dorothea he had seen it on numerous occasions, with and without other people, and whenever he saw the form he never heard a sound but on other occasions he heard the sound of her footsteps and could follow her progress by this means, sometimes inside his home and sometimes in the garden, but when he heard her he saw nothing and when he saw her he heard nothing. Dorothea St Hill Bourne told me they watched the figure for several seconds; it seemed to be taking a leisurely walk, its head somewhat bowed as though she was looking at the ground, but otherwise upright and elegant and totally unaware of their presence. Within a very short while she seemed to shiver or shimmer and the next second she was no longer there. Both Dorothea and Paul Getty went to the spot where they had seen her but there was no sign of her or anything to suggest she had been there and certainly nowhere she could have gone. Paul Getty seemed quite unconcerned, presumably used to seeing the form, and he said his servants and bodyguards had often seen the form and he had noted that when anyone approached the form, it seemed to shiver – as they had just seen it do – and then disappeared. It was not always seen in the same place in the garden and it had been seen in various parts of the interior of the mansion.

Within this truly magnificent mansion for sixteen years in succession, towards the end of his life, Paul Getty personally entertained Christmas parties of up to fifty children from broken homes, leading a chorus of 'Jingle Bells', dressing up as Father Christmas, taking part in egg and spoon races across the richly-carpeted floor and pulling crackers and handing out presents to everyone. It was an annual occasion that he seemed to really enjoy. 'I love to see the children playing happily in my home,' Getty said on one such occasion. 'They are so fresh and honest. No asking or looking for favours: this is one of the rare joys of my life' – but not the only joy surely . . . Memories flood in of other wonderful parties such as the one on 31 July 1960 that Getty gave for Miss Jeanette Constable-Maxwell when dinner for a hundred people was served on gold and silver plates and there was a sumptuous buffet of lobster and caviar. 'Easily the most fabulous evening since the war,' said one visitor. 'Quite social, eh?' Getty himself commented.

Paul Getty, arguably the wealthiest man in the world, was married five times, his first three brides, all teenagers, he married within five years; the fourth attempted suicide within months of the marriage; yet I found him a timid, reclusive man, very afraid of fire and disliking travel, especially flying. Soon after the First World War he had his first flight in a little plane and as soon as they were airborne the pilot found something wrong and said, 'Mr Getty, we have to go back'. When they landed Paul Getty alighted from the plane and never willingly got in another. He was known for his meanness, even charging his son when he came to lunch and installing a pay-phone for the use of guests but this was not a characteristic I encountered.

In fact when I first wrote to him about the possibility of bringing some friends with an interest in ghosts and ghostly happenings to Sutton Place I was not a little surprised to receive a reply asking when I could go and see him. I did so and found this shy and quiet man more than willing to talk about ghosts and soon he readily agreed to a visit and among those I selected to accompany me on that occasion were F. R. Maude OBE, Dr Letitia Fairfield, Granville Squiers, Eric Wookey MC, Lietenant-General Sir Kenneth Lock, Colonel R. C. Morris, mediumistic Muriel Hankey and Hope Alexander, former Head of Copyright at the BBC – the latter I recall could hardly believe I had organised a visit to Paul Getty's home, but like everyone else I invited, she came!

I remember the enormous fireplaces, the grand high-ceilinged rooms, the magnificent oak table once owned by William Hearst, the priceless Brussels tapestries, the Old Masters, the gold candelabra and amid it all the slight, almost frightened, figure of the man whose father was a devout Christian Scientist and who in common with his son was always deeply superstitious. When an American psychic told Paul Getty that he would die on foreign soil he sent confidential letters to a number of his friends in different parts of the world asking them to ensure that he was sent to his home in California if he ever looked like dying in their part of the world. Two of his sons predeceased him and while he does lie buried in California beside them, as was his wish, he died 6,000 miles away, virtually alone, wrapped in a blanket in his study at Sutton Place.

As he showed me round the interior of Sutton Place, where the Duke of Windsor wrote of being alone in a 'huge room which felt spooky'; the place one of Paul Getty's grandsons described as 'dark and gloomy and scary', I recall so well as he was telling me about the unidentified ghost in the Long Gallery, mentioned by a visitor as long ago as 1777 (and by another visitor in 1980!) we looked at each other as loud crashing sounds suddenly accompanied us as we walked and preceded us as we entered the Great Hall. Paul Getty gave me one of his rare smiles and said 'The ghosts are welcoming you too!'

I must emphasise that the quite tremendous noise seemed to originate from just beyond the door we were about to pass through, yet on entering the Great Hall there was nothing whatever to account for the startling sounds and the enormous room was patently devoid of any human beings. During our group visit a few weeks later something very similar happened and was witnessed by upwards of a dozen responsible people; while in the haunted garden two of the party independently reporting to me that they had 'almost' seen a fleeting form that sped with remarkable agility behind a bush and then completely disappeared. Both thought they saw a white human-sized form out of the corner of their eye and when they turned to see what it was 'something' white seemed to speed behind a bush and there completely disappear.

Now, I understand, Sutton Place is in the possession of yet another American millionaire and I await with interest any reports from him of supernormal activity in his beautiful and haunted garden.

TAN-YR-ALLT
Tremadoc, Gwynedd, Wales

During the course of research for my *Ghosts of Wales* (Chris Davies, 1978 and Corgi, 1980) my wife and I were invited to visit Captain S. Livingstone-Learmouth who told us he lived in a haunted house with a haunted garden.

Before venturing deep into the lofty rocks and magnificent woods of the area, we explored first Tremadoc and found the house, Woodlands, at the southern end of the town where T. E. Lawrence, 'Lawrence of Arabia', was born in 1888 and we stood in the garden where to the south the waters of Portmadoc bay shimmered and to the north the green foothills rose slowly to the peak of Snowdon: a fitting beginning perhaps for the man who was to live an adventurous, triumphant, sad and lonely life. He was without doubt one of the major mysterious personalities of all time – and his ghost walks in the garden of his beloved Clouds Hill, as we have seen.

Three-quarters of a mile from Portmadoc, sheltering under great rocks and hiding amid luxurious trees and bushes, we found the long, low, white verandaed

house called Tan-yr-Allt and charming Sandy Livingstone-Learmouth was there to greet us and welcome us into the house where eccentric Percy Bysshe Shelley (1792-1822) had lived for a time in either 1812 or 1813 with Harriet Westbrook and where he wrote some of his influential 'Queen Mab'. At all events the man who is regarded as one of England's greatest lyric poets seems to have left his mark here for a mysterious figure in a long grey cloak and wearing what looks like a tricorn hat has been seen in the garden here by various people including Sandy and his wife, on separate occasions and also together, crossing the garden from the big windows that look out on to the lawn.

Interestingly enough when Shelley was at Tan-yr-Allt he became convinced that his revolutionary ideas and championing of various insurrectionary movements had resulted in the government sending someone down to Tremadoc to keep an eye on him. One night he saw a man looking in at him through the big windows and Shelley grabbed a gun and took a shot at the intruder, unfortunately he forgot to open a window first and so caused quite a mess! The incident is interesting in as much as Sandy Livingstone-Learmouth also saw a man looking in through the window one night and when he fetched his wife they both saw the figure of a man in a long grey cloak and wearing a peculiar three-cornered hat in the garden on the same side of the house on several occasions and Sandy has always wondered whether it was this same phantom form that Shelley saw – unless, wondered Sandy, the figure he saw was Shelley himself! He certainly loved Tan-yr-Allt and we were shown a plaque on the veranda commemorating the fact that he wrote most of his poem 'Queen Mab' there: 'Queen Mab' with its haunting lines: 'How wonderful is Death/ Death and his brother Sleep.'

Sandy Livingstone-Learmouth went to live at Tan-yr-Allt in 1947 and he soon suspected that the place was haunted. Footsteps were frequently heard walking along an upstairs passage; windows rattled when there was no breath of wind; doors opened and closed by themselves – or, as Sandy put it, 'it seemed to me then that the house, after dark, was full of footsteps.' Once he remarked to his wife (who died in 1952) that 'the place must be haunted'; she was most annoyed at the idea but could not deny that on several occasions they had seen a figure in the garden that seemed to have no rational explanation, a figure that disappeared in quite inexplicable circumstances and, curiously enough, after her death Sandy was alone in the house one evening when he heard a car go past the door of the house, which puzzled him. He heard the same thing four nights in succession and on the fifth night it stopped. Years before Sandy had taught his wife the old motorist's trick for an easy start: rev-up, apply choke and switch off. It was something his wife always did and as the car stopped outside the house that fifth evening Sandy was astonished to hear this procedure followed, exactly as his wife would do and had done thousands of time. Sandy went into the hall to see who was there. The drive in front of the whole of the house was clearly visible but there was no sign of any car there, nothing. As he stood in the hall, the old Jack Russell terrier dog and his wife's cat both advanced to the centre of the little hall, sat down in unison, turned their heads and apparently watched something invisible pass through the closed front door and proceed into the house. Usually the dog would bark his head off at any car that came near the house –except their own – but on this occasion both the dog and the cat were subdued and quiet: it was almost as though their mistress was coming back to settle things and indeed some of the unexplained noises ceased after that episode.

Just once Sandy saw a manifestation of his wife and on several occasions he heard her footsteps walking towards her bathroom; the old terrier heard them too and watched with great interest; and once a close friend, artist Kyffin Williams, and Sandy both heard the footsteps and saw the bathroom door open and close by itself.

Even as Sandy Livingstone-Learmouth relived these odd happenings and related his experiences in the house and in the garden and also something of the history of the house, we all heard an occasional sudden rattle, a snatch of music, a footfall or two in the empty house and deserted garden and drive and also the hint of a whisper from nowhere. 'It is a happy house,' I put in my notes at the time, 'with a grand atmosphere but the air seems full of secrets and it breathes history.'

There is a small farm above the house, Pant Ifan, that Sandy has let for many years to the Birmingham Cave and Crag Club ('grand fellows') for a peppercorn rent: 50 pence a year and, 'a gallon of sound ale'. One day the local practitioner, Dr Brothers, was on the bottom road when he chanced to look up and saw a man fall off the top of a very conspicuous rock, known as Hound's Head. He distinctly saw the man fall about 200 feet, hit some branches of a tree with a sickening crash and disappear into the undergrowth with a thud. The police were alerted and a search party combed the whole area but they didn't find even a broken branch let alone a man.

Some years previously something of the same kind had happened when more than a dozen people in Tremadoc were convinced that some climbers had fallen and hurt themselves in the woods near Tan-yr-Allt. Then too, the police were involved and search parties, including fifty-two actual climbers, conducted a thorough and lengthy search, without finding any trace of an accident.

'The external haunting here is a very benevolent one,' Sandy told us. 'Usually the modus operandi is this: one hears a lot of shouting, chattering, laughing and the sound of voices although one can never identify any words and as soon as one goes to look carefully across the lawn and into the woods, all noises stop completely – except for a great gale of laughter on occasions . . .'

We left Tan-yr-Allt warm with the friendship of Sandy Livingstone-Learmouth and more than satisfied that we had visited a haunted house with a haunted garden.

WESTEINDE 12
The Hague, The Netherlands

A haunted house on the Westeinde, one of the higher parts of The Hague, was for many years the British Embassy and in the 1960s the British Ambassador, Sir Peter Garran, was kind enough to give me full details of the house and the ghosts and it is from what he told me that I detail this remarkable story. With previous appointments in Belgrade, Lisbon, Berlin and Washington and Ambassador to Mexico from 1960 to 1964, Sir Peter, with his wealth of experience with all sorts of people in all parts of the world said he had never come across anything like this and the 'unique story really began 500 years ago when the Hall of Knights in the centre of The Hague was a hunting lodge of the counts of Holland.'

Apparently they held their hunting parties in the Hague Woods (which were then very much more extensive than they are today). In those days there were three or four great sand dunes running roughly south-west to north-east, with marshy areas between them. One is now Sportlaan, the next the Laan van Meerdervoort and then comes the Westeinde. Possibly a farm house once stood where the embassy house now stands, just as there was once a farm house on the site of the Noordeinde Palace. The earliest record of the embassy property is to be found in the first surviving Court Book of The Hague dated 1458 which records one Gerrit van Assendelft as being in possession of 'the houses which stand between the Lorrestege and the Jan Heynriczsstraet, the gardens included'. For these houses and gardens this Gerrit van Assendelft was due to pay a small annual rent to the Count of Holland of eight denarii.

Three years later it is recorded that on 8 February 1461 Gerrit van Assendelft conferred his house on Pieter van Darn, Abbot of Middelburg, and by letters patent of 20 February received it back as a fief, or feudal tenure, for which he was required to pay a yearly sum of eight denarii to the abbot – the same amount that he was paying by way of rent to the Count of Holland.

This Garrit van Assendelft was a man of substance and his house on the Westeinde had come to be known as the House of Assendelft. He was a counsellor of Charles the Bold and of Kaiser Maximilian; and he married a wealthy heiress named Beatrix van Dalem, and in the Council Chamber of the Grote Kerk, just a hundred yards away from the House of Assendelft, there is a fine marble tomb that contains the mortal remains of Gerrit himself, who died in 1486, and of his wife Beatrix, who died six years later.

We do not know much about what the house looked like in those early days. Only the cellars remain, to form the foundation of the present building, but they are proof enough that it was a substantial structure. There were said to be underground passages leading from these cellars to the Grote Kerk. Gerrit's son, Nicholas, who inherited the house, also made a good marriage with Alyt van Arckel, Lady of Kyeffhouck and Cralinghen. She survived him by thirty years and shared the inheritance with her son Ridder Gerrit van Assendelft who, as a young man, at the beginning of the sixteenth century, went off to France to study law in Orléans, where he met and married a girl named Catherine de Chasseur. This was a disastrous match and led to tragedy. It seems to have been something of a shotgun wedding – she was the daughter of an innkeeper – no doubt of the inn where young Gerrit lodged while he was in Orleans. She was apparently an attractive girl and the lonely young Dutchman was not yet twenty years of age and one can imagine the rest. The account I have read runs as follows: 'He had married her against his will, or rather under pressure from her father who, when he found them together, forced them to get married in the presence of notary and witnesses.' Just how angry and upset his mother, the proud Alyt van Arckel, was about this we can only imagine.

When young Gerrit returned to Holland he tried to leave his wife behind in France, but she followed him to The Hague, and when he refused to admit her to his house, the Court – the Hof van Holland – of which he was later to become president; taking no account of rank, state or fortune, ordered him 'to take her to live with him in his house, at his table and in his bed.' But it did not work. His mother and his sister Catherine did all they could to turn him against his wife and their child, Nicolaes or Claes. His mother did not live to see the results of her intrigues. She died in 1530 and two years later the marriage broke up. There was a legal separation and Catherine left the house in the Westeinde under a settlement by which she was provided with a house at the corner of the Voorout and the Nieuwstraat and an allowance of Fls. 600 a year, plus the cost of bringing up young Nicolaes.

Gerrit for his part had come to be a man of considerable importance and influence. He had also become a favourite of the Emperor Charles V, and he was for thirty years, from 1528 to 1558, President of the Court or Hof van Holland. Even so, Catherine de Chasseur in her house in the Nieuwstraat, is said to have lived 'above the rank and state of her husband', and obviously very extravagantly. To make ends meet she took to counterfeiting money, with the help of her French chaplain, Mathurin Alys, and two other young Frenchmen. On 11 February 1541 she was caught red-handed with her accomplices. There was clearly a great public scandal. The wife of the President of the Court of Holland, although separated from her husband, caught forging money! Catherine was tried and condemned to death. The original sentence was that she should be burned in public at the stake, but by special mercy of the Queen of Hungary, then Regent of the Netherlands, her sentence was commuted to private execution in prison and burial in consecrated ground – some slight compensation, perhaps, for being the lawful wife of an important citizen. It is a recorded fact that Catherine de Chasseur was executed on 11 April 1541 in the Gevangepoort by the gruesome method of the water death – being filled with water until she expired. Her accomplices were beheaded.

Gerrit van Assendelft, after his wife's death at the hands of the executioners, determined to cut his son Nicolaes out of his inheritance. He had indeed to give his son his 'legitimate portion' but why leave to this child of 'a woman of poor and humble origin' all his titles and extensive properties? He hit upon the idea of urging and persuading his son to go into the priesthood, and in this he succeeded, with the help of various friends. He then petitioned the Emperor Charles V for an 'octrooi' – an authority – to leave his titles and most of his properties to two of his brothers and their heirs – on the plea that he wanted to preserve the family titles and the family properties, now that his son had become a priest, and could not therefore help with the inheritance. He received the required 'octrooi' and made a will, perhaps with a slightly uneasy conscience, first in favour of two of his brothers. Then, when his brothers died before him, he made a new will in favour of two nephews, their children. He died himself at the age of seventy, in 1558, a lonely man in the great house on which he had left his mark by many changes and improvements, and we are told that the great bell of the Grote Kerk rang out dirges in his honour for three days before his burial.

On Gerrit's death, his son Nicolaes upset all the deep-laid plans of his father. He sought the Pope's consent to renounce his vows on the grounds that he had only joined the priesthood under pressure. This was duly granted and he then proceeded, with considerable success, to lay claim to his father's properties. He married a wife, but had no children by her. Curiously enough, the two nephews to whom his father had bequeathed his properties and titles also died childless. This did not, however, prevent the development of a terrific family feud. After all, there were a lot of titles and a lot of properties. Nicolaes, and after his death in 1570 his great-nephew Floris, who was his heir, seem to have remained in effective possession of the Westeinde house, but the 'have-nots' among the Assendelft relatives could not reconcile themselves to this. There were claims and attempted settlements and finally a tremendous law suit. All the family scandals came out in the evidence, and eventually, in 1645 – eighty-seven years after old Gerrit died – a judgement 130 pages long finally declared old Gerrit's will invalid and confirmed the co-lateral heirs of his son Nicolaes as the rightful owners of the van Assendelft titles and properties, including the House of Assendelft. This judgement was confirmed on appeal in 1656, ninety-eight years after old Gerrit's death. And all this happened because of the inkeeper in Orléans who insisted on the young law student Gerrit van Assendelft marrying his daughter, Catherine de Chasseur.

Meanwhile in 1574 the town of Middelburg had fallen to the siege of William the Silent's armies and the States of Zeeland had taken over the properties of the Abbey of Our Lady of Middelburg, including the House of Assendelft. The house itself then seems to have been extensively altered, probably by a great-nephew of Nicolaes van Assendelft and the tenure passed to a van Assendelft daughter, Anna, widow of Gerald van Renesse van der Aa, and it was rented to various people, the most important of whom was Johan de Witt, First Minister of the United Provinces. Up to that time, 1653, he had stayed in The Hague at the Logement van Dordrecht, with the other representatives of the town of his birth, but on becoming Grand Pensionary it was considered desirable for the sake of 'dignity' that he should come and live in the great house on the Westeinde, although he had to borrow money from his uncle for the purpose. And so he lived there for two years from 1653 to 1655, when he married Wendela Maria Bicker and bought a house of his own on the Kneuterdijk. Then, in 1677, Vrouwe Anna's son, Georg Frederick de Renesse, Lord of Assendelft and Baron of Elderen, sold the house. The purchaser was the Spanish Ambassador to The Hague, Don Emanuel Francisco de Lyra, in the name of the King of Spain and so this Huis van Assendelft became the Spanish Embassy. That was, of course, some twenty-nine years after the end of the Eighty Years War. De Riemer's book, *Beschrijving van 's-Gravenhage*, records that the house in those days had a huge garden stretching out behind it and that in fact only the Noordeinde Palace had a larger and finer garden in the whole of The Hague. De Riemer goes on to describe a huge fountain in the middle of the garden that spouted water high into the air and was fed from a reservoir on the roof of the house.

To return to the house: in 1754, or by some accounts three years later, the Spanish Ambassador of the day had the old house pulled down and built the existing 'residence'; and the strange thing is that, apart from the arms of Philip V of Spain, which still stand over the archway, there is nothing Spanish about the house. It seems a typical Dutch town house of the period with French (Louis XV) influence.

Then came the Napoleonic wars and the occupation by Napoleon's armies of both the Netherlands and Spain. In 1811 the King of Spain was in exile and short of money and he gave orders for the house to be sold. It was bought by Petrus Judocus van Oosthuysen, Lord of Rysenburgh, one of the wealthiest men in The Hague and a pious Catholic, who is said to have acquired the house to save the chapel. He did not live in the house, but rented it out and then in 1832 the house was bought by a certain Chevalier de Gilles of Antwerp, who six years later presented it to the Jesuit fathers but they never lived in the house which, after twenty years as the Danish Legation, was rented for another eighteen years, from 1843 to 1861, by the Minister of Prussia, Count von Konigsmark.

Then in 1861 Sir Andrew Buchanan, who was British Minister at The Hague, took a lease of the house, probably for a twenty-one-year term for a rent of Fls. 3,000 a year. This lease was renewed again and again and again. So, Westeinde 12 has a history that is traceable back to 1458. The old house changed hands first by inheritance within the Assendelft family and then passed through marriage to the Renesse family, until it was bought in 1677 by the King of Spain and became the Spanish Embassy. The existing house, in the 212 years of its existence seems never to have had any other occupant than the head of a diplomatic mission. A remarkable pedigree for a haunted house with a haunted garden! Few, if any, other houses in the world can match this record. The British, Sir Peter Garran told me, have been proud and happy to have the house first as their Legation and, since the Second World War, as their Embassy for well over 100 years. Sir Peter was the twentieth British incumbent and so far as he knew the only other British Residences that can claim a longer occupation are in Paris and Copenhagen; and an interesting coincidence is that the minister who negotiated the first lease of the Legation in Copenhagen was Sir Andrew Buchanan.

Everyone who has lived in the house on the Westeinde has found it a very pleasant house although some have found the house 'probably' haunted and the garden 'certainly haunted'. Sir Horace Rumbold, who was minister from 1888 to 1896, wrote in his memoirs: '... in some respects it was the most interesting house I ever occupied in the many changes in my career...' There have been persistent references over the years to the presence of ghosts in the house and in the garden. Again Sir Horace Rumbold writes: 'upstairs... there ran a long, dark corridor with a number of good-sized bedrooms opening onto either side, some of which we made as bright and liveable as we could, without however entirely succeeding in divesting the passage itself of a depressing gloominess for which it was difficult to account. Vague stories were indeed current of the building being haunted, and the occupants of one room in particular were certainly plagued by vivid nightmares which, through the recurrence in them of the same distinctive features, were singularly akin to spectral visitations. There is, I am told, no doubt that my successor in the house found it advisable to give up using the room in question as a bedroom and turned it into a boxroom.

Be this as it may, we were all of us from the first conscious of an undefinable atmosphere of creepiness and mystery pervading the entire rambling building after dark'. The garden seems always to have had a creepy reputation and there are numerous reports of inexplicable figures being seen and spooky happenings occurring. Sir Horace continues: 'Towards the end of my tenancy I became aware of the gruesome and thoroughly authentic tradition attaching to the house; records that still exist in the State Archives at The Hague . . .'

One of the ghosts would appear to be none other than Catherine de Chasseur, the French girl from Orléans, whose unhappy story has already been told. The suggestion that the 'spirit' of Catherine de Chasseur comes back to the house where she was once happy can hardly be correct because her relations with her husband, Gerrit, in the old house must always have been difficult. But at least she enjoyed a rank and prestige in the house which she could never otherwise have known and perhaps that could still mean a great deal to her restless spirit, Sir Peter mused, besides she had reason to be anxious about the fate of her son, Nicolaes.

Actually the first known reference to a ghost comes in a letter to Johan de Witt from his sister Johanna. It was Johanna who took on the task of getting the house ready for her brother when he came to live there in 1653. On 16 August of that year she wrote to him from Dordrecht for advice: the girl she had engaged as a kitchen maid, Grietien, was unhappy at the prospect of sleeping alone in the house 'because she had heard tell that both house and garden were haunted' and Johanna asked whether Grietien might spend the night with Juffrouw Verbies or Major de Veer.

A wealth of manifestations were reported in the years that followed. Sir Horace does not specify which room was the one in which sleepers had 'vivid nightmares which were singularly akin to spectral visitations' but Sir Peter thought it very probable that it was the small room at the end of the passage, over the archway. It would be interesting to know what form those nightmares took. And there is much talk of a spectre being seen in the garden, sometimes visible from the house and at other times encountered, when least expected, in the garden.

There is also reference to a ghost in a book by Meriel Buchanan, the daughter of Sir George Buchanan, who was Minister in The Hague from 1908 to 1910. Miss Buchanan states; 'two maids in succession left us, complaining that somebody, or something, had tried to pull the covers off their bed in the middle of the night and they had seen forms they could not explain in the garden. Once, I experienced the same sensation myself and although I turned on the light immediately no one was there. I did hear the rustle of a dress, as if someone had hurriedly left the room . . .' From then on there are a succession of stories about ghosts and ghostly happenings inside the house and outside in the garden but they are difficult to check up on.

There are many references to 'watery manifestations', which could be links with the way Catherine de Chasseur died. We can speak with more authority, says Sir Peter, of the time when Sir Odo Russell was minister, from 1928 to 1933. During his time there were many manifestations or indications of the presence of a kind of poltergeist: doors opening and closing by themselves, things taken from drawers and scattered around the floor, water lying about in unexpected places, and taps inexplicably turned on. The Russell children had no doubt whatever about an unseen presence in that small room at the end of the passage already described. This was known, at that time, as the Train Room, because the youngest of the children, David, had his toy trains there. One day David, alone in that room, was quite certain that the 'presence' was between him and the door. He finally made good his escape, but he never wanted to play with his trains there again. Perhaps the most remarkable manifestation of all occurred one evening in the dining room when the table was ready for a large dinner party and suddenly, just before eight o'clock, water poured from the ceiling, falling exactly in the place where the hostess was to sit. The table itself had to be hurriedly removed to the ballroom and reset, but the strangest thing of all was that afterwards there was no sign of water damage to the ceiling. In the garden too there are several instances of a mysterious female figure and the appearance of water where there should be no water.

In the time of Sir Paul Mason (1954-1960) his small son, Will, once saw a lady with her head covered walking the upstairs passage and once outside in the garden he saw the same figure. No explanation was ever found for her appearances. Then there was the English girl living with the Masons; one evening while alone in the house she was taking a bath in the bathroom on the Westeinde side of the 'haunted' passage with the Mason's corgi dog, an inveterate barker, for company. She suddenly saw the corgi crouch back, all hackles up, dead quiet and obviously very frightened, and at the same time the girl heard footsteps and saw the handle of the bathroom door turn. The door was locked. There was no sound of footsteps going away yet when she was sufficiently brave to unlock and open the door, there was nothing to be seen. The dog behaved in the same way several times in the garden although nothing was visible to its human companions to account for its behaviour.

Have they seen the ghostly lady themselves, I asked Sir Peter and Lady Garran. 'That is not easy to answer,' Sir Peter replied. 'But one evening, and strangely enough on the evening of a day when a Jesuit priest had come to tea, while my wife and I were sitting at dinner, something shadowy seemed to pass between us. I saw what looked like a waving line of smoke which moved slowly across the table. My wife did not notice anything and I cannot offer any logical explanation for it. It could have been the misty outline of a full and flowing dress. Curiously enough our butler, Brinkman, who served at the embassy for over forty years, also believed that he once saw the ghost and when my wife asked him next morning what it was that he had seen, Brinkman, not knowing about my experience, said "a shadowy figure with a grey and smoky skirt". He claimed to have seen something very similar in the garden on two occasions.'

During their sojourn at the house on the Westeinde Sir Peter and Lady Garran entertained Princess Margaret and Lord Snowdon and previous visitors included the Prince of Wales (later the Duke of Windsor), Winston Churchill (no stranger to ghosts), Queen Juliana of The Netherlands and Prince Bernhard and their daughters.

It is known that structural alterations and the presence of certain people can promote psychic activity and the house and in particular the garden at this interesting house do seem to have been permeated with the potential for psychic happenings over many years. It could well be that the story of hauntings here is not yet complete.

THE WHITE HOUSE
1600 Pennsylvania Avenue, Washington DC, USA

Several ghosts have been reliably sighted, both inside this historic house, the first government building to be constructed in Washington, and outside in the gardens; nearly a dozen at the last count, but as someone once said somewhere, that has not – so far – stopped anyone from running for President! In particular the phantom form of Abraham Lincoln has long been reported to frequent the rooms and corridors; and beautiful Abigail Adams has been seen in the garden.

President Theodore Roosevelt maintained that he often felt Lincoln's spirit and saw the ghost of the great man on many occasions, usually in the room where Lincoln once slept, now known as the Lincoln Room. In the second-storey room where Willie Lincoln died of typhoid fever in 1862, witnesses have repeatedly heard a clattering sound, thought to be the sound of their son Tad Lincoln's goats pulling their master on a chair around the East Room. In the same room disembodied voices and the sound of weeping have been heard on occasions. It was in the East Room too that Lincoln had the precognitive dream of his own assassination and where he subsequently lay in state. Franklin D. Roosevelt too believed he had encountered the ghost of Lincoln in the East Room.

Roosevelt was fascinated by the stories of Lincoln's ghost and one of his maids told him she had clearly seen the figure of the lanky President sitting on the edge of the bed pulling on his boots one morning Her screams brought some secret service agents and ushers running to her assistance but the room was, of course, empty by the time they arrived.

Franklin Delano Roosevelt had an open mind on the subject of ghosts and the possibility of contact with the spirit world. He once told his wife: 'I think it is unwise to say you do not believe in anything when you can't prove that it is either true or untrue. There is so much in the world which is always new in the way of discoveries that it is wiser to say that there may be spiritual things which we are simply unable to fathom.'

When Carl Sandburg was preparing his biography of Lincoln he went to see Roosevelt and asked him whether he knew in which room of the White House

Lincoln had spent most of his time. The President replied that he didn't know for sure but he had always felt that it had been the Blue Room, overlooking the Washington Monument. Sometimes, when he was there alone, he added, he could have sworn that Lincoln was present.

When the show *Watch on the Rhine* was performed at the White House, the negro actor Frank Wilson had a private chat with the President after supper and they talked about the ghost of Abraham Lincoln. 'Mr Wilson,' the President said. 'The spirit of Lincoln still lives on here.' On another occasion a group of Broadway entertainers were being shown the various famous rooms at the White House by the President's wife, Mrs Eleanor Roosevelt and when they reached the Lincoln Room, Patricia Bowman, the ballet dancer, said she felt the room was definitely haunted. Mrs Roosevelt then admitted that she had always felt so too and just a few days previously a maid, Mary Eban, had seen the ghost of Lincoln in the same room.

At one time Mrs Roosevelt commented on the Lincoln legend during the course of her New York *Daily News* column, 'My Day', and she suggested that any place where someone had lived really hard would be quite likely to be haunted by their personality.

Mr J. B. West was the chief usher during the Truman administration and he has spoken of the mysterious creaks and groans and knockings heard in various parts of the White House during the Truman years: sounds for which there could never be found any logical explanation. There are reports that President Truman, although a sceptic, himself encountered the ghost of Abraham Lincoln at the White House – on more than one occasion.

In 1956 ex-President Harry Truman revealed that when he was at the White House he got up from his bed several times in the middle of the night to answer raps upon his bedroom door but never found anything or anyone there; his daughter Margaret has said she too had heard unexplained raps in one of the bedrooms during the middle of the night.

On one occasion Katurah Brooks was working late at night in the Rose Room on the second floor when she was startled by a sudden burst of laughter, loud and booming. When she looked up she saw, just for a moment, the figure of Abraham Lincoln. The ghost of the great American President has also been seen walking through the East Room and standing thoughtfully at the window of the Oval Room, looking out towards Virginia; Mrs Coolidge, wife of the 13th president, was one more dependable witness for the apparition of Abraham Lincoln at the White House.

The ghost of Lincoln's son, Willie – whose spirit the President believed was constantly with him – was seen by several members of the White House staff during Grant's presidency and after the assassination of President Lincoln on 14 April 1865 a phantom train – no less – is reported to have appeared each April on the New York Central Railroad at Albany, New York. It was the funeral train retracing its slow and melancholy journey from Washington to Illinois. The event was reported in the *Albany Evening Times* where it was stated that railway workers would make a point of sitting along the track in the early evening of 27 April to wait for the train that reportedly appeared for several consecutive years.

It may be significant that both Abraham Lincoln and Franklin Roosevelt held séances at the White House. Soon after Lincoln became president he was shown an article in *The Cleveland Plain-dealer* suggesting that he accepted the possibility of spirit return. He said in reply: 'This article does not begin to tell the wonderful things I have witnessed. Half of it has never been told'. During the presidency of Franklin Roosevelt a medium was flown regularly from the West Coast to the White House during the anxious war years; many séances were held and both presidents seem to have sought the guidance of the spirit world in affairs of state.

Queen Wilhelmina of the Netherlands, while staying at the White House, heard a knock on her bedroom door during the night. She got up to open it – and promptly fainted. Hearing of this state of affairs next morning the President enquired about the matter, expressing some concern. 'I know it sounds ridiculous,' Queen Wilhelmina responded. 'But when I opened the door I saw Abraham Lincoln standing there. Then everything went black and I fell to the floor.' Other ghosts at the White House include those of William Henry Harrison, the 9th US President who died only a month after inauguration. His ghost was frequently seen wandering about the attic area in the days before the White House was rebuilt during Theodore Roosevelt's administration.

Outside the most frequently reported ghost is that of Abigail Adams (1744-1818). Abigail lacked formal education, in common with many women of the period, but she read avidly and it was reading that created a bond between her and young John Adams (1735-1826), a Harvard graduate set on a career in law but destined to become the second president of the USA. They married in 1764 and it was a marriage that endured for more than half a century. When she was fifty-six she was painted by Gilbert Stuart, considered to be one of the finest portraitists of the day, and he is reported to have told a friend that he wished he had had the opportunity of painting Abigail Adams when she was young for he believed she would have been a perfect Venus. Always dignified and tactful, she was remarkable in many ways, not least for being the wife of one president of the US and the mother of another.

The ghost of Abigail Adams has long been positively identified gliding noiselessly through the Long Hall and disappearing through the double-doors of the East Room. Some witnesses say she appears to be carrying loads of laundry to hang in the East Room – as she probably did in her lifetime since she moved into the President's House before the property was completed and the East Room was the driest area in the house. The phantom form of a young and beautiful Abigail Adams has also been seen, with arms outstretched in front of her, walking towards the present White

House as she must have done, amid the muddy, unpaved and uncultivated garden as she knew it.

Dolley Madison (1768-1849) moved into the White House in 1809 when her husband, James Madison, was elected 4th President of the United States. His periods of office were stormy ones which included the war with England from 1812 to 1814 and when British troops captured Washington and burned the White House, it was the 'famous and charming' Dolley who saved Stuart's celebrated painting of George Washington and the original draft of the Declaration of Independence. For half a century Dolley Madison was the most important woman in the social circles of America and to this day she remains one of the best known and best loved ladies of the White House; nothing could disturb her happy personality and her warm heart, exquisite manners on all occasions and her charm and dignity, which she never lost; and she enjoyed the deep respect of her friends and her country to the last.

Among her many virtues, Dolley (as she always spelt her name) was very keen on gardening and she planned and built the beautiful Rose Garden at the White House and perhaps it is appropriate that her gentle ghost has been seen times without number in the vicinity of the Rose Garden but especially during the administration of Woodrow Wilson a hundred years after it had been so carefully and lovingly planned and planted when Mrs Wilson gave orders for it to be dug up. Almost immediately workmen reported the ghost of Dolley Madison appearing in the garden and keeping them from their work and in fact preventing any demolition of the beautiful Rose Garden. After that no one dared to interfere with the White House Rose Garden and the ghost of Dolley Madison, according to reports, still returns periodically to ensure that all is well.

Interestingly enough the ghost of Dolley Madison is also seen in the garden of the Dolley Madison House on the corner of Madison Street, Washington, where Dolley spent her last days. James Madison died in 1836 and for practically the whole of the remaining thirteen years of her life Dolley lived at the Madison Street house. Her ghost, sometimes seen in a rocking chair, became so famous that gentlemen leaving the nearby Washington Club late at night would invariably raise their hats to the ghostly Dolley Madison who was, apparently, as charming and presentable as a ghost as she had been in the flesh. Her ghost has also been reported at the Octagon (where the Madisons lived while the White House was being rebuilt) invariably accompanied by the scent of lilies, one of Dolley's favourite flowers.

The ghost of a British soldier from the war of 1812, who died in the White House grounds, is also said to haunt the White House gardens occasionally, carrying what appears to be a torch in his hand; while other reported ghosts at the White House include that of Andrew Jackson, while witnesses for the restless ghost of Abraham Lincoln include Lady Bird Johnson, Theodore Roosevelt, Grace Coolidge, Dwight D. Eisenhower and Margaret, the daughter of Harry Truman.

WINCHESTER MYSTERY HOUSE
525 South Winchester Boulevard, San Jose, California

Described with some justification as 'the world's largest, oddest building', in fact enormous and very, very curious, Winchester Mystery House might accurately be described as a monument to death.

Sarah Winchester, heiress to the Winchester rifle fortune and the last of the line was one of the most remarkable women in the history of the American West. The famous repeating rifle may have been known as 'the gun that won the West' to the pioneers but to Sarah Pardee Winchester (c. 1840-1922) the weapon was an instrument of death, doom and destruction – ultimately for herself. The widow of the rifle manufacturer's only son, following the death of her husband and baby daughter, she went to see a medium, Adam Coons, in Boston, where she was convinced she spoke with her dead husband who informed her that the spirits of all those killed by Winchester rifles had placed a curse upon her and her only way to evade the curse was to sell her property in the east and move west and there build a house, adding rooms to shelter the ghosts of the ever increasing number of victims of Winchester guns and as long as building continued the spirits would be appeased and she would escape the curse.

The deeply unhappy heiress promptly moved to California and there succeeded in purchasing a house that was under construction which she then proceeded to alter, remodel, reconstruct and add to – for as long as she lived! She moved there in 1884 and died there in 1922 and all the years she lived there she never entered another building or church, never rode on a bus or a train, never paid a friendly visit to anyone, nor did she accept visitors or pose for photographs and anyone calling at Winchester House was coldly informed by a resplendent but austere butler, 'Madame is indisposed'. Eventually the front door was permanently locked, then boarded up and it was never used again. Very occasionally, as, for example, when she was forced to leave her home for a while, after the San Francisco earthquake, she used her own carriage – and once, as she returned home, a gardener, hiding in the bushes in the garden, took a photograph: it is the only known photograph of Sarah Winchester and would undoubtedly have been destroyed and the photographer punished, if she had ever known about it.

During the thirty-eight years she resided at Winchester House Sarah held nightly séances in the small and secret Blue Room hidden in the middle of the house and in accordance with the capricious and insatiable instructions she received from the 'other side' she employed hundreds of workmen on a round-the-clock basis, including Sundays and holidays, to build the required room after room, balcony after balcony, chimney after chimney, stairway after stairway and doorway after doorway until today 160 rooms can be located in this baffling labyrinth of a place – the survivors of an estimated original 750 chambers that were often pulled down as soon as they were built to make way for new rooms, passages and stairways: anything as long as building continued.

Every night, at midnight, a melancholy bell summoned the shades of the dead to come to her nightly meetings and it is said there were frequent dinner parties and banquets held in the Gold and Silver Dining Hall with Sarah presiding over honoured phantom guests. At two o'clock in the morning the bell tolled again and the ghosts departed until the bell summoned them again – or so Sarah Winchester said. On her death Sarah left all her possessions to her favourite neice, Marion Merriman, with strict instructions to see that the ghosts of yesteryear would continue to be made properly welcome to the house. Eventually Marion Merriman sold the house, making sure the new owner knew all about Sarah Winchester's interests and beliefs.

Today the aptly named Winchester Mystery House contains literally miles of winding, twisting and bewildering passages and corridors that snake through the house often ending in closets from which there is no escape or exit or else there is suddenly a solid wall. It has been said that the house was devised by ghosts for ghosts and perhaps that is true. It used to be thought that ghosts liked to vanish up chimneys so Sarah provided them with not one, not two, not half-a-dozen, but no less than forty-seven chimney escape hatches at Winchester House.

In her early days at the mystery house Sarah invariably enjoyed a vintage wine with her evening meal but one evening when she went to the wine cellar to select a bottle she saw, to her horror, a distinct and indelible black handprint on the wall, yet only she possessed a key to the wine cellar. That night the spirits told her it was the print of a demon's hand. Sarah took it to be a warning against alcohol and she had the cellar

walled up and concealed so thoroughly that the liquid treasure house has not been found to this day.

At Winchester Mystery House the number 13 predominates, for Sarah was convinced that the number had a potency to check bad spirits; thus chandeliers have 13 lights, the Carriage Entrance Hall has 13 cement blocks, there are 13 blue and amber stones in the Spider Web Window, ceilings and walls have 13 panels, rooms have 13 windows, there are 13 bathrooms and 13 steps into each, 13 hooks in the Blue Room, 13 gas jets in the Ballroom chandelier, many of the stairways have 13 steps and there were even 13 parts to her will and her signature appears 13 times!

Locked in her ever-growing monstrosity of a house, the wealthy Sarah taxed her wits to confuse the bad ghosts: she never slept two consecutive nights in the same bedroom; built scores of skylights to dispel the shadows of the spirits; built exit doors to look like cupboard doors to fool the ghosts, together with switchback staircases, small doors alongside normal ones, stairs that led nowhere, a herringbone flooring that provided an optical illusion, the suppression of mirrors (only two in 160 rooms), pointed roofs and a thousand other things she thought might deter unwanted spirits.

Whether or not the activities of Sarah Winchester and her builders have any bearing on the fact, it does seem indisputable that the house and garden are ghost-ridden to a remarkable degree with inexplicable footsteps, indistinct whispering, the distinct sound of rattling chains, indisputable cold spots and icy draughts, unexplained balls of red light and phantom forms that are likely to be encountered anywhere at any time. 'To be alone in this place during the day is not so bad,' author Susy Smith says. 'But a certain chill seems to be in the atmosphere . . . and no one would want to be left there after dark . . .'

The gardens are equally as mysterious and strange and haunted as the house. One of the first jobs given to the twelve gardeners was to plant a high hedge around the entire property; Sarah Winchester wanted no one, not even those in her employ, to see what she was doing. Some of the gentle garden paths lead nowhere, paths are intertwined and exotic trees of all kinds stand guard over ornate fountains that have played water into the sky twenty-four hours a day. In the garden too is a statue of a Red Indian chief, depicted firing arrows at hidden enemies; it was created by Sarah as atonement for the many thousands of peaceful Red Indians who had been killed by bullets fired from Winchester rifles. Each day, rain or fine, Sarah visited the gardens, strolling along the winding paths, making changes and ordering new work.

Today visitors to the garden have reported hearing strains of organ music. Sarah Winchester was once a good musician but her hands became so afflicted with arthritis that she could hardly hold a pencil, let alone play the organ, and no living person in the house would dare touch the instruments. One visitor described his tour of the house and garden as 'like wandering through the corridors of a schizophrenic mind!'

The phantom form of Sarah Winchester has reportedly been seen on many occasions in the garden, occasionally accompanied by a man. Both are dressed in clothing popular at the turn of the twentieth century. Could it be Sarah and her garden manager discussing new ideas, as they did so many times a century ago? Perhaps they approve the appearance of the restored Victorian statuary, greenhouses and other outside features, never before open to the public but now available to everyone.

Among the personal accounts of unexplained experiences of past and present employees, guests, visitors and psychical researchers preserved by the directors at the Winchester Mystery House are a number of incidents relating to the garden.

Brent Miller, caretaker from 1973 to 1981, has told of 'an unearthly and mysterious silence', 'the sound of someone breathing' and footsteps that have no human origin. Arlene Bischel reported the unusual experience of losing her eyesight after visiting several rooms; outside in the garden, sitting on a bench in the sun for a while, she regained her sight. Twenty-three years later Mrs Bischel paid a return visit but experienced nothing out of the ordinary. Mike Bray, a tour supervisor, has told of hearing a soft voice whispering his name when there was no human being in the house or in the garden. Kelsey Harding, another tour guide, was in the south conservatory conducting a tour when one of the sloping windows blew open and then slammed shut, breaking the window. There was no wind at the time and nothing like this has ever happened before or since. There are too many first-hand instances of the feeling of being watched, of following footsteps, and unrecognised phantom forms, and locked doors being opened, and lights being switched on or off, and of lights in the house being seen to be on when viewed from the garden and then off and then on again when there is nobody inside the house.

Manifestations in the garden also include a ghostly man in overalls and, especially interesting, a small, grey-haired lady and Sarah Winchester was under five feet tall. The figure appeared to be dressed in long black clothes such as Sarah used to wear and witnesses have remarked upon the passing resemblance to Queen Victoria in her later years. During her lifetime people who saw Sarah Winchester described her as not unlike Queen Victoria. One investigator has concluded that 'scores of people, including staff and visitors' have encountered ghosts at Winchester Mystery House where paranormal activity has been recorded at all times of the day and night. No wonder the management maintains a file of affidavits signed by witnesses who have experienced strange happenings at this strange place.

One visitor told me she and her husband visited Winchester House one warm and sunny day but while walking through the garden they both suddenly felt distinctly chilly and at the same time they both simultaneously saw the figure of a small and elderly woman walking authoritatively along a path ahead of them. She appeared to be dressed in very out-of-date clothes and the visitors' first thoughts were that a tour guide was dressed for the part but then, as suddenly as they had seen her, the figure vanished completely and the atmosphere resumed its warm air of summer. Both the visitors had been looking at the figure when it vanished and they could hardly believe their eyes. They went to the spot immediately but could find no explanation then or later for the sudden appearance and equally sudden disappearance of the seemingly solid figure in the haunted garden at Winchester Mystery House.

Sarah Winchester was eighty-five when she died, having lived nearly half her life in her lonely sepulchre, amid building operations of one sort or another every single day. For Sarah Winchester the house and the garden was an enchantment, as it still is, and that could well be what she intended all along.

SELECT BIBLIOGRAPHY

Alexander, John, *Ghosts: Washington's Most Famous Ghost Stories* (Washington Books, 1988)

Armitage, Flora, *The Desert and the Stars* (Faber and Faber, 1956)

Atkins, Meg Elizabeth, *Haunted Warwickshire* (Robert Hale, 1981)

Broughall, Tony, *Ghosts of Bedfordshire and Hertfordshire* (unpublished manuscript)

Cartland, Barbara, *I Seek the Miraculous* (Sphere, 1979)

de Lisser, Herbert, *The White Witch of Rosehall* (Benn, 1936)

Flower, Raymond, *Meet You at Raffles* (Times, Singapore, 1988)

Godden, Rumer, *A House With Four Walls* (Macmillan, 1989)

Green, Andrew, *Ghosts of Today* (Kaye and Ward, 1980)

Hauck, Dennis W., *National Directory of Haunted Places* (Athanor, Sacramento, 1994)

Harper, Charles G., *Haunted Houses* (Cecil Palmer, 1907)

Haynes, Renee, *The Society for Psychical Research – A History* (Macdonald, 1982)

Hole, Christina, *Haunted England* (Batsford, 1940)

Howard, Leslie Ruth, *A Quite Remarkable Father* (Longmans, Green, 1960)

Huxley, Elspeth, *Peter Scott – Painter and Naturalist* (Faber and Faber, 1993)

Hyde, H. Montgomery, *Story of Lamb House* (Adams, 1966)

Jones-Baker, Doris, *Folklore of Hertfordshire* (Batsford, 1977)

Karloff, Boris, *Tales of Terror* (World Pub. New York, 1943)

Klapthor, Margaret, *The First Ladies* (White House Hist. 1955)

MacGregor, A. A., *Phantom Footsteps* (Robert Hale, 1959)

MacKenzie, Andrew, *Hauntings and Apparitions* (Heinemann, 1982)

Mais, S. P. B., *Lovely Britain* (Odhams, n.d.)

Marriott, Paul & Yvonne Argent, *The Last Days of T. E. Lawrence* (Alpha Press, 1996)

Matthews, Rupert, *Haunted Cambridge* (Pitkin, 1994)

Moreno, Francisco, *Toledo* (Editorial Everest, Leon, 1970)

Norman, Diana, *The Stately Ghosts of England* (Muller, 1963)

Onieva, Antonio, *Complete Guide to the Prado Gallery* (Editorial Mayfe, Madrid, 1976)

Routh, C. R. N., *They Saw It Happen* (Blackwell, 1956)

Smit, Tim, *The Lost Gardens of Heligan* (Gollancz, 1997)

Squiers, Granville, *Secret Hiding Places* (Stanley Paul, 1934)

Stirling, A. W. M., *Ghosts Vivisected* (Robert Hale, 1957)
–, *The Merry Wives of Battersea* (Robert Hale, 1956)

Underwood, Peter, *Gazetteer of British Ghosts* (Souvenir, 1971)
–, *The Ghost Hunters* (Robert Hale, 1985)
–, *Ghosts of Hampshire* (St Michaels Press, 1981)
–, *Ghosts of Somerset* (Bossiney, 1985)
–, *Ghosts of Wales* (Davis, 1978)
–, *Ghosthunters Almanac* (Dobby, 1993)
–, *Guide to Ghosts and Haunted Places* (Piatkus, 1996)

–, *Hauntings* (Dent, 1977)
–, *A Host of Hauntings* (Leslie Frewin, 1973)
–, *Nights in Haunted Houses* (Headline, 1994)
–, *This Haunted Isle* (Harrap, 1983)

Underwood, Peter and Paul Tabori, *The Ghosts of Borley* (David & Charles, 1973)

Wales, Tony, *Sussex Ghosts and Legends* (Countryside, 1992)

Zachary, Frank, *Rose Hall*, Jamaica (Kingston, 1973)